Great Separations
"And God Separated" (Genesis 1:4)

Book I of the Kalmus Series
Cho Larson

Albertville, AL

Published by Warner House Press of Albertville, Alabama USA

Copyright © 2021 Cho Larson
Cover Design and Illustration © 2021 Ian Loudon, OKAY Media
Interior Design © 2021 Warner House Press

All rights reserved. No part of this book may be used or reproduced in any manner whatsoever without written permission, except in the case of brief quotations in critical articles and reviews. For more information, contact

Warner House Press
1325 Lane Switch Road
Albertville, AL 35951
USA

Published 2021
Printed in the United States of America

Cover image used under license from Shutterstock.com.

Unless otherwise noted, all scripture quotations are taken from HOLY BIBLE, NEW INTERNATIONAL VERSION®. Copyright © 1973, 1978, 1984 by International Bible Society. Used by permission of Zondervan Publishing House.

Scripture quotations marked ESV are from The Holy Bible, English Standard Version®, Copyright © 2001 by Crossway Bibles, a publishing ministry of Good News Publishers. Used by permission. All rights reserved.

Scripture quotation marked NRSV are from New Revised Standard Version Bible, copyright © 1989 National Council of the Churches of Christ in the United States of America. Used by permission. All rights reserved worldwide.

Scripture quotations marked NLT are from the Holy Bible, New Living Translation, Copyright © 1996, 2004, 2007, 2013, 2015 by Tyndale House Foundation. Used by permission of Tyndale House Publishers Inc., Carol Stream, Illinois 60188. All rights reserved.

26 25 24 23 22 21 1 2 3 4 5

ISBN: 978-1-951890-20-9

Contents

The Starting Line...iii

Chapter 1: Revealed in Creation...1

Chapter 2: The Word of Creation..7

Chapter 3: Great Separation Sequels..................................29

Chapter 4: The Pathway of Light...43

Chapter 5: The Measuring Rod..57

Chapter 6: I Can Do It..71

Chapter 7: Fire of Separation..79

Chapter 8: Body, Soul, and Spirit Work Together 95

Chapter 9: Gates and Walls of Separation.........................107

Chapter 10: The Benefits of Separation..............................15

Chapter 11: Pass Over the Thresholds..............................125

Chapter 12: Today and Forever..133

Chapter 13: The Finish Line in Sight.................................139

Postscript...150

Acknowledgments...151

About the Author...153

*"To preach the gospel,
and not with words of eloquent wisdom,
lest the cross of Christ be emptied of its power."*
The Apostle Paul[1]

---

1. 1 Corinthians 1:17 ESV.

The Starting Line

Like each stride in a marathon, the pages of this study are steps toward the finish line in the Great Commission race. It's a racecourse that any man, woman, or child who seeks God's kingdom may prepare for. These words are timely for all who hear the heroes of faith cheering them on,[2] and for all who will push forward, to press on to the finish line. This race cannot be run in the strength of common man, but in the strength of the Spirit. To run in His strength, we are called to separate what is holy from what is common. We must "consider loss for the sake of Christ"[3] our God-given common strength and abilities and step up into the power and strength of the Holy Spirit.

Great Separations is the first book of the Kalmus[4] Series. This study builds on the tenets of the four books of the Kingdom Series.[5] It's a course designed to prepare you to run the race. This study was prepared for those who desire to do the work Jesus assigned to us before He ascended to the Father. The message of this book is vital, because what you train for today is preparation for all eternity.

> *The world and its desires pass away,*
> *but the man who does the will of God lives forever.*
>
> (1 John 2:17)

As modern-day Christians, we tend to ask the LORD to strengthen *us* to accomplish *our* dreams and goals. All too often, we mistake common for sacred because our experiences feel spiritual. We allow common things to replace what is holy because of the blessed feelings that come over us in special moments of life. It feels like a divine moment to walk hand in hand on the beach at sunset as you watch God paint the sky with vibrant colors on the horizon. A sense of awe comes over us as we watch our newborn son take his first breath. Our hearts feel as if they will burst, filled with love as we gather to celebrate with children and grandchildren around the Thanksgiving table. These are all special, God-given blessings for our life here on earth, but they are not holy. They are not sacramental. Yes, cherish the special moments of life and give thanks to God for them, but we must not confuse them with what is holy.

---

2. Hebrews 12:1–2.
3. Philippians 3:7.
4. Kalmus: Rabbinic Aramaic for "quill" (pen) is from the Greek "kalamus" meaning "reed" (an alternative to the quill as a writing instrument).
5. Kingdom series books: *Hearts for the Kingdom, Treasures of the Kingdom, A Jewel of the Kingdom,* and *Kingdom of Grace.*

The concept of separation runs counter to our present-day culture that desires all people in the world to live in harmony. We want everybody to love everyone—and we ought to. We may think separations are in conflict with peace on earth, but in reality, God's separations make a way for the Prince of Peace to rule on earth. The separations in this study do not create a divide. Instead, they are like leaving father and mother to become united in marriage. Likewise, the purpose of this *Great Separations* study is to separate us from limitations and weaknesses of the common realm. The goal is to separate us to Christ, and the power of the cross of Jesus Christ, for the work of the church and the Great Commission.

In this crazy world, we have all witnessed separations that are crucial. As an example: to be safe, we separate ourselves from abusive people. We separate ourselves from toxic relationships. In a much greater way, God delivers us and separates us from sin that would destroy us physically and spiritually. God breaks away those things that would short-circuit our relationship with Him, who has adopted us as His sons and daughters. Indeed, God's good separations restore us to relationship with our Heavenly Father.

As God's children, we are called to separate ourselves to God, who is holy. In our study, we will give extra attention to this area of greatest confusion. That is, God-given common gifts and talents that are often confused with the spiritual gifts given by the Spirit for the work of the church. We will learn why common dreams, strengths, achievements, and goals should no longer be our focus as we worship, minister, and serve. This study encourages Christians to seek God Almighty to strengthen them in spirit and step into God's dreams—His eternal purpose and plan. To accomplish this goal, we will approach the topic of separating holy and common from several different viewpoints.

We'll start with Moses, who penned the words of the Pentateuch: "In the beginning." The Apostle John began to write his Gospel with the first epistle proclaiming, "In the beginning." The Gospel of Luke begins by taking us all the way back to the first man, Adam, in its genealogies. In the book of Job, God settled the matter of Job's trials by taking him back to Earth's creation and asking him, "Where were you when I laid the earth's foundation?" Jesus took the Pharisees back to the beginning to answer their question about divorce. The writer of Hebrews takes us back to the creation of Earth to prove the deity and authority of Jesus as High Priest of a New Covenant. The Apostle Paul brought order to gatherings for worship by taking the people back to the day Adam and Eve were created.[6] In Paul's letter to the Colossians, he established the supremacy of Christ, revealing Jesus as "the firstborn

---

6. 1 Corinthians 11.

of all creation."[7] When God spoke through the prophets of old, He spoke with authority as Creator. For the same reason, the foundation of this study is: "In the beginning."

It is I who made the earth and created mankind on it.
My own hands stretched out the heavens; I marshaled their starry hosts.

(Isaiah 45:12)

For today's Christian to understand essential Biblical principles, it is important to know our Creator's nature and to see God's imprint upon all His creation from the beginning. For us to grasp the concepts of this natural realm, the kingdom of light, and the kingdom of darkness, our eyes must be opened to see God in all His majesty as Creator of all the heavens and earth. In this, we will see Creator God as holy.

"Holy, holy, holy is the Lord God Almighty," who was, and is, and is to come.

(Revelation 4:8)

By contrast, God created common light on the fourth day for a natural, everyday purpose. This light separated daytime from nighttime, determined the seasons to grow and harvest, and marked time as it passes—blessings for all humankind.

He causes his sun to rise on evil and the good,
and sends rain on the righteous and the unrighteous.

(Matthew 5:45)

Light and darkness, day and night are obvious distinctions. The genesis of these clear-cut demarcations leads us to understand how important it is to know that God is light and God alone is holy. Once this distinction becomes clear, we can separate what God established as holy, and what He made to be common. What is common is good, given by our Father in heaven to all His creation to provide for and sustain life. What is holy is built upon the Cornerstone, Christ Jesus, to build what is eternal. This separation of holy and common is difficult because they often work together. God uses what is common to direct our eyes to what is eternal and holy.

"Common," as used in this study, is like the sand of the seashore. God set the sand on the shoreline in place for His good purpose: to give the waters of the seas a boundary they cannot cross.[8] While the common sand of the seashore serves a good purpose, it is not holy ground. Holy, in this study, is defined by the Hebrew word קָדוֹשׁ qadosh: to be separate, set apart, and con-

---
7. Colossians 1:15.
8. Jeremiah 5:22.

secrated. As this study progresses, we will see that what is common cannot be used in place of what is holy. Also, throughout the study, you'll find the word "order." This is order that God established each day of creation. Creation's orderly foundation continues by means of Christ, the living and active Word, to provide order for the stars and planets, the seasons of the earth, social systems, families, churches, and civic and economic structures. God's established order in creation is the foundation for, and the test by which truth is established. What the Almighty brought into being in seven days is a great test for what is written in this study.

One of the primary themes in this study is a call to step up to the greater work the church is called to accomplish in this season. While this change may be a difficult adjustment where strong, established paradigms exist, it is possible in Christ.

Throughout history, God has used whom He chooses to accomplish His work in the world. For His purpose, the Lord God selects people from within the church and in the community, whether or not they are Christian. The Holy Spirit, in our day, has accomplished the work of the Spirit with God's people as they minister and serve in their common gifts to do the work of the church. In this way, God accomplished His purpose and plan. Now the Lord will prepare us to do a new thing, or rather, God will once again prepare a people who will minister and serve by means of the anointing, gifting, and empowering work of the Spirit of Jesus. This is His call for us to minister Jesus' living and active presence to push back sin's darkness in the world.

The LORD Almighty is an awesome, holy and righteous God. There is none other like Him—no one who compares to Him in any way. God spoke through the prophet Isaiah, saying:

> *I will not yield my glory to another.*
>
> (Isaiah 42:8)

Yet the Church, God's people, in our day too often minister and serve by means of common gifts alone. They use what is common to accomplish what is better accomplished by the power, anointing, and gifting of the Spirit of Jesus. Our attempts to do the work of the Great Commission by means of what is common diminishes what can be accomplished, and we take away from God's glory. Today, God is calling His people to, once again, minister the living, active presence of our Lord Jesus to a world steeped in darkness. We are once again called to minister in the power of His holy name, and in the power of the Spirit of Jesus. This is an important point because this eternal work cannot be accomplished any other way. In this way, God receives all the glory and honor that is due Him.

This is the reality of the matter: Will we do the work of the kingdom of heaven in the strength of the first Adam, or in the power and strength of the last Adam, Jesus Christ? Will we run this race by means of what is made from the dust of the ground, or will we run by means of the Spirit of Christ who came from above?[9]

Why is this separation of holy and common so important now, in this day? Because the work of the Great Commission cannot be completed by common means alone, or in the strength of common man or woman. When reading and studying the Scriptures, a sense of urgency will come over us. God's word compels us to look toward the finish line of the Great Commission race. Our feet may start to drag as we trudge toward the goal. And yet the strength we need comes by means of the anointing, gifting, and empowering work of the Spirit. There is no power in mortal beings to accomplish what is only possible in the Spirit. The race we are in today may be likened to a runner who catches his second wind, and then sprints to the finish line. Start out in the little strength you have, but catch the wind of the Spirit for the final sprint.

To win the race, we are called to separate holy from common. A topical study is the best method for training us to run. It's essential to keep in mind the importance of balance, even in our training methods. As Christians, we become spiritually healthy when we have a balanced spiritual workout. This strengthens us to partake of the fullness of Christ—all that He offers to build us up and all He promises to make us fit for this work with eternal effect.

Some churches are strong on expository teaching, with verse-by-verse instruction through the Bible. I've grown spiritually from this kind of teaching. Other churches have a three-year lectionary to teach through the Scriptures, and this is also an excellent way to partake of the whole message of the Bible. And yet, we also gain many benefits when we chew on choice morsels from God's Word—this is topical teaching. *Great Separations* is not intended as a whole and balanced diet, but a choice morsel—one course in a great feast.[10]

This study book is intended to focus on some of the facets of our faith that too often are left behind, like Brussel sprouts on the buffet table. Teaching to reveal a holy and righteous God in an impossible task—but in Christ all things are possible. Likewise, it is impossible for the reader to grasp hold of these truths except by the Spirit of Truth who reveals it. Please begin this study with prayer, or better yet with fasting and prayer.[11]

---

9. Weigh this in light of 1 Corinthians 15:45–49.
10. A more balanced menu is presented in the author's book, *Hearts for the Kingdom*.
11. A study on fasting is found in *Hearts for the Kingdom*, Chapter 17.

First, we will observe the work of God Almighty as Creator of all heaven and earth to see Him in all holiness. We'll see that the Genesis separations were just the beginning of God's covenant works with all He created. Our study Scriptures will help us see the light of righteousness of Jesus Christ and its powerful effect. We will discover the measure of God's holy possession, and the immeasurable fire of the Spirit of Jesus.

In this study, we'll come to know the work of God's fire that separates us to Christ for the work of the church. This study teaches us why light and darkness, holy and common, and righteousness and self-righteousness cannot be mixed in the same recipe. We will confront strongholds in our Christian walk and in the church that limit us in our Christian calling.

We will work toward these goals as we study what God has separated and why He separated as He created for seven days of creation and thereafter. What are we separated from? Unto what are we separated? In the kingdom of heaven, what are the gates and walls that separate? What thresholds must we cross to be separated for God's good purpose? How do body, soul, and spirit work together in light of separation principles? In all the separations, we are joined together in Christ—and we will see how God accomplishes this good work in all who are called out of darkness into His glorious light. We'll learn about the ways that God's separations benefit us in our Christian ministry and service.

Finally, we will apply the same truths of Scripture about what God has made holy to the ministries of spiritual gifts and the empowering work of the Spirit of Jesus in the church today. This truth will become evident as we go forward, and we will see why the ministries of spiritual gifts are holy, unlike common gifts.[12] We will learn about spiritual poverty that comes when we discount the ministries of spiritual gifts that God has declared to be holy.[13]

My approach to the study of this topic is like adding up Scripture upon Scripture. A + B = C. "A" is what we see revealed in God's miraculous creation. "B" is what the Scriptures reveal to us about God of our salvation. This equals "C," what God makes known to us when these truths come together in agreement. As an example: **A:** We know that God reveals Himself to created beings in all that He has created.

> *For since the creation of the world God's invisible qualities–his eternal power and divine nature–have been clearly seen, being understood from what has been made, so that people are without excuse.*
> (Romans 1:20)

---
12. 1 Peter 2:5.
13. A complete study on spiritual gifts, how they are gifted by the Holy Spirit, and the ministries of gifts can be found in the author's books: *Treasures of the Kingdom*, *A Jewel of the Kingdom*, and *Kingdom of Grace*.

Add to this truth, **B:**

But you are a chosen people, a royal priesthood, a holy nation, God's special possession, that you may declare the praises of him who called you out of darkness into his wonderful light.

(1 Peter 2:9)

This equals **C:** What God has revealed about His sovereignty over what is holy and what is common. Read on for the rest of the answer.

My hope, as you get into this study, is for God's Word to be opened to you. Dig in just like you would search through the operator's manual for your shiny new truck. Add to this the oil of the Spirit and your heart will be opened to understand.

Our prayer: LORD, open our eyes to see our sin and our depravity. LORD, break our hearts because of our earthbound attitudes and our corrupt hearts. LORD, bring us to confess with our mouths our sin and our need of Christ. Change our hearts. Change our minds and conform us to your image so we cannot be separated from the power of Christ and the cross of Jesus Christ.

Chapter 1: Revealed in Creation

Key Scripture:

- "The heavens declare the glory of God; the skies proclaim the work of his hands. Day after day they pour forth speech; night after night they reveal knowledge. They have no speech, they use no words; no sound is heard from them. Yet their voice goes out into all the earth, their words to the ends of the world." (Psalm 19:1–4)

To know God, who is holy, by any means other than the revelatory power of the Spirit of Christ is impossible. To know God in our heart of hearts is beyond the reach of common men or women. Knowledge of the fullness of God is beyond the grasp of human intellect. The purpose of this chapter is to inspire you to reach out in spirit and touch the heart of God Almighty, to encourage you to separate yourself in Christ Jesus,[1] and to come with reverence and awe to worship God in spirit and truth. When you come to know Him, you will be compelled to answer the call to be separated to God who is holy. When separated from the world's darkness, you will come to know the Word, that is, Jesus Christ the Light of the world, who spoke and all things were created.

The height of the heavens, the immeasurable vastness of the universe reveals to us the sovereignty of God: His majesty, His glory, His fearsome radiance, His splendor, beauty, and holiness. His awesome presence and His nature are declared to us in all He has created. He is God who reigns above all and over all He has brought into existence. These attributes are revealed in all He created. God's beautiful creation came into being as God separated. He began by separating light from darkness—because He is holy. The Hebrew word for holy is קָדַשׁ *qâdash*, meaning to set apart, to separate, and separateness. Therefore, a holy God spoke into being all the heavens and earth, and the elements of creation were separated from chaos and set in order. The order God established in seven days of creation, by means of Christ the Word, continues to provide a path for stars and planets, the seasons of the earth, social systems, families, churches, governance, and economic structures. God's nature is revealed when we see His established orderly separations. When this truth becomes clear, we will see that His heart overflows with love toward us who are made in His image.

---

[1]. "Be holy, because I am holy." (1 Peter 1:16).

The first book of the Bible, Genesis, reveals the Father, His heart, His nature, His love, His mercies, His saving Grace, and His plan of salvation. Genesis reveals the Word—God's only Son as Redeemer. Genesis reveals God's unchanging purpose. God created man and woman and gave them a job: to fill and subdue the earth. Read through the Bible and the accounts of many who overcame, all the way to the last book, Revelation, where you hear God's command to the seven churches to be victorious and overcome. This is the same command given to Adam and Eve in the beginning. God's plan has not changed.

For us, the Church, we come into strength when we come to know God's orderly creation that is evident in family, church, and the Good News Gospel. When we understand God's orderly creation, as revealed in Genesis, our worldview will change. An inspired "light bulb" moment will open our eyes to see the Creator revealed in the first words recorded in the Scriptures.

When time began in Genesis, we see the Alpha revealed. Before this, no time existed—only eternity. In the beginning, God "created." This is the Hebrew word: בָּרָא *bara'*. The connotations of this word are: to cut down, to shape, to polish, and to transform.

The true meaning of "create" is brought to light in Jamieson, Fausett & Brown's commentary on Genesis 1:2: "The earth was without form and void—or in 'confusion and emptiness,' as the words are rendered in Isaiah 34:11. This globe, at some undescribed period, having been convulsed and broken up, was a dark and watery waste for ages perhaps, till out of this chaotic state, the present fabric of the world was made to arise."[2]

As we understand God's nature, revealed to us starting with day one of creation, the world around us starts to make sense. When we begin to grasp God of creation, we will come to understand the purpose of God's commands. The blinders come off and the lights turn on. The veil is torn away, for God has made a way for us to come near to Him, to dwell in His dwelling, to bow in His presence, and to stand in His council, free from the penalty of the Law. The LORD Almighty is perfect in holiness.[3] He is faithful to all He spoke into being as He created the heavens and earth, and His holy presence holds this created universe together.[4] How do we come to know that our Creator is holy? It's an important question because the creation is only possible by means of a holy God.

---

2. Robert Jamieson, Jamieson, Fausett & Brown. 1871. "Text Commentary." Available on https://www. blueletterbible.org/commentaries/jfb/.
3. **Holiness**, as used in this study, is the Hebrew word קֹדֶשׁ *qôdesh,* ko'-desh. It means: apartness, sacredness of God, set-apartness, and separateness.
4. Colossians 1:17.

We have all heard humorous statements like, "You know you're a missionary when a bug lands in your coffee and it makes you happy." Maybe you'll relate to this one: "You know you're a mom when a trip to the grocery store by yourself is a vacation." We have fun with these statements, but now let's move on and complete this sentence: "I know God is holy because _____." We have to get beyond the Sunday school answer, "Because the Bible says so." It's important for us to become aware of God's holy presence. This awareness must soak deep into our soul and spirit, and not be limited to intellectual knowledge alone. This truth must penetrate into our heart of hearts. My hope is to bring you to stand shoulder to shoulder with Job to say with him:

My ears had heard of you but now my eyes have seen you.

(Job 42:5)

With every creative word spoken into the chaotic mass called Earth, we come to see and to touch the heart of the Lord Almighty. The Word of creation brought into being an earth that reveals the glory, majesty, splendor, radiance, and beauty of a holy God. In our day and time, we can come into agreement with this awesome creation by separating ourselves to God who is holy. When we do this, our work, family, community, society, and government will follow suit and come into order. The Creator's harmonious order makes it possible for us to fill and subdue the earth as He commanded. Indeed, every word of creation reveals a loving heavenly Father, His grace, His love, His mercies, and His plan of salvation.

Chapter 1
Revealed in Creation
Q & A

1. How has this study session enriched your concept of this created world?
   _____
   _____
   _____

2. What is revealed in the first chapters of Genesis about Creator God? How does this affect your view of the world around you?
   _____
   _____
   _____

3. What words best describe the harmony of creation and its good purpose?
   _____
   _____
   _____

Our prayer: Oh, LORD. Open our eyes.
Open our hearts to know you in all your splendor and holiness.

My Journal Notes

Chapter 2:
The Word of Creation

Key Scripture:

- "By the word of the LORD the heavens were made, their starry host by the breath of his mouth. He gathers the waters of the sea into jars; he puts the deep into storehouses. Let all the earth fear the LORD; let all the people of the world revere him. For he spoke, and it came to be; he commanded, and it stood firm." (Psalm 33:6–9)

An overview of each day of creation reveals the significance of order-creating separations. The holiness of God Almighty is revealed with each separation. In this study, we'll see the Creator's "separations" repeated in each of the seven days. This study session will help us grasp hold of the truth that the Almighty spoke to bring harmony to the Earth's chaotic mass.

We'll learn that the harmonious order of creation set the foundations of the earth for all time. The Creator separated out of darkness, the water above from the water below, the dry land from the water, day from night. He created the creatures in the sea, the birds that fly above, living creatures were separated from the dust of the ground, and finally the first people were created to inhabit the garden. To learn the great significance of God's separations, this study gives extra emphasis to the days of creation that most clearly reveal the Creator's holy nature.

Creator God displays His great purpose as He creates all the heavens and earth. Consider that God's perfect creation is a great gift, given to humankind for our good. He created Earth as a perfect home with a bountiful table. Adam and Eve lacked for nothing. They found joy in the work of tending the garden. Their walks with God in the cool of the day were certainly an awesome delight. Can you imagine the fellowship they shared as Father God encompassed Adam and Eve who walked hand in hand with their Creator? Each day of God's creation opens our eyes to see more of His holy nature.

Day One

On the first day of creation, God separated light from darkness. He began the work of creation with Earth's sphere as a watery, chaotic mass. But God transformed this primordial mix as He separated to make order out of chaos for seven days. God separated Light from Darkness as the first work of creation. The word used for "light" on the first day of creation is the Hebrew word אוֹר *'owr*. This is more than light for the natural eye to see. It is light for the heart.[1] Jesus spoke of this light when He said:

> *I am the light of the world.*
> *Whoever follows me will never walk in darkness, but will have the light of life.*
>
> (John 8:12)

The God of Creation dwells in this unapproachable light, and coming near Him (or the angels who come from His presence) produces fearful trembling. Who then can approach God Almighty? Those who are wrapped in the righteousness of Jesus Christ may come in boldness. Those who separate themselves from the righteousness of Jesus Christ will be too terrified to approach, but for those who walk in the light there is great hope. The prophet Isaiah wrote of this truth:

> *The sinners in Zion are terrified; trembling grips the godless:*
> *"Who of us can dwell with the consuming fire?*
> *Who of us can dwell with everlasting burning?"*
> *Those who walk righteously and speak what is right,*
> *who reject gain from extortion and keep their hands from accepting bribes,*
> *who stop their ears against plots of murder and shut their eyes against contemplating evil–*
> *they are the ones who will dwell on the heights,*
> *whose refuge will be the mountain fortress.*
>
> (Isaiah 33:14–16)

When we see this vast chasm between the God of Light, as revealed in God's creation, and the darkness in our hearts, we see our corrupt state and must acknowledge our need of Christ. By the work of the cross of Jesus Christ, this gap is bridged and we are brought into fellowship with a holy, awesome God—Creator of all the heavens and earth. When we see God's mercy shown to fallible creatures of His creation and His loving, caring nature, we are drawn to His light. The light of the first day of Creation is an eternal. It displays the light of Christ. Meditate on the following verses to see the first day's light revealed:

> *The light shines in the darkness, and the darkness has not overcome it.*
>
> (John 1:5 ESV)

> *If then your whole body is full of light, having no part dark,*
> *it will be wholly bright, as when a lamp with its rays gives you light.*
>
> (Luke 11:36 ESV)

---

1. The difference between the light of the first day of creation (אוֹר *'owr*), and the fourth day (מָאוֹר *ma'owr*) is as different as the wind that rustles the leaves and the wind of the Spirit. (John 3:8; 20:22)

> *Take no part in the unfruitful works of darkness, but instead expose them.*
> *For it is shameful even to speak of the things that they do in secret.*
> *But when anything is exposed by the light, it becomes visible, for anything that becomes visible is light. Therefore it says,*
> *"Awake, O sleeper, and arise from the dead, and Christ will shine on you."*

(Ephesians 5:11–14 ESV)

On the first day of creation, light and darkness were separated. The Apostle Paul quotes Genesis 1:3: "Let light shine out of darkness."[2] Light and darkness confront us every day of our lives. Joshua spoke of the battle we face with light and darkness:

> *Choose this day whom you will serve.*

(Joshua 24:15)

He presented the people with a choice: God's kingdom of light, or the kingdom of darkness. As God placed Adam and Eve in the Garden of Eden, they were confronted with the tree of life, or the forbidden tree of the knowledge of good and evil. God gave Adam a clear and simple command:[3]

> *And the Lord God commanded the man,*
> *"You are free to eat from any tree in the garden;*
> *but you must not eat from the tree of the knowledge of good and evil,*
> *for when you eat from it you will certainly die."*

(Genesis 2:16–17)

But they were like children told they could play in the yard, but to stay out of the street. All of a sudden, the hot pavement looks more attractive than the soft, cool grass in the yard. Adam and Eve chose darkness and, as a result of this, all their progeny, all who come after them are born with a debt of sin. Because of this, every child born on earth must be called out of this enslaving darkness. We have no power of our own to be separated from sin's darkness—this is the work of the cross of Jesus Christ.

> *He brought them out of darkness, the utter darkness, and broke away their chains.*

(Psalm 107:14)

We can best understand the light and the darkness that confronts us when we become aware of God's work of creation. On the first day of creation, God made clear demarcations between the light of righteousness and the chaotic

---

2. 2 Corinthians 4:6. From the Greek on this verse it could be paraphrased:
  "Let light be separated from, and taken out of darkness."
3. For an expanded teaching on the two trees, see *Treasures of the Kingdom*, by Cho Larson; Chapter 2, page 18.

darkness that permeated "the face of the deep." As stated before, the Hebrew word (אוֹר *'owr*) means light as created on the first day. This light is greater than the lights of the fourth day (מָאוֹר *ma'owr*). The Hebrew word for "light" of the first day includes heavenly luminaries, but it is so much more. It's the light of prosperity, light as God's garment, the Light of the World, the light of instruction, the light of God's holy nation, light for life's pathway, the light of the Gentiles, the Light of Life, the Light of Christ, and the light of God's presence.[4] This is the eternal light of the New Jerusalem.

This everlasting radiance contrasts with the forth day's natural light, ἥλιος *hḗlios*, for all human eyes to see. It's a φωτίζω *phōtízō*, light that causes something to exist, and enlightens us with knowledge of the Almighty Creator. This is infinite light, λύχνος *lýchnos*, to shine out on the citizens of God's kingdom by means of His glory.

> *The city does not need the sun or the moon to shine on it,*
> *for the glory of God gives it light, and the Lamb is its lamp.*

(Revelation 21:23)

We can grasp the significance of the first day's light when we get a sense of the darkness that pervaded the earth before being driven back. But where did the darkness come from?

> *I form light and create darkness, I make well-being and create calamity,*
> *I am the Lord, who does all these things.*

(Isaiah 45:7)

In this verse, we learn that:

- God formed the light and created the darkness.
- God is sovereign over darkness.
- Light in the context of this Scripture is defined as "well-being" and the darkness as "calamity."

To apply this truth regarding the separation of light and darkness, keep in mind that in the light of the first day is the radiance of Christ. As God's servants, we are called to separate ourselves in the light of Christ. This foundational Genesis truth affects every area of our lives because the reality of Christ's light compels Christians to separate themselves from the material world's dark side.

---

[4] Light of prosperity: Isaiah 9:2, Psalm 97:11. God's garment of light: Psalm 104:2. The Lord is light: Micah 7:8. Light of instruction: Proverbs 6:23. Light of the face: Exodus 34:29. Light of God's holy nation: Isaiah 10:17; 60:1–3. Light for life's pathway: Psalm 119:105. Light of the Gentiles: Isaiah 49:6; 51:4. Light of life: Psalm 56:13. Light of Christ: John 1:4; 8:12. Light of God's presence: Psalm 89:15.

> *No servant can serve two masters,*
> *for either he will hate the one and love the other, or he will be*
> *devoted to the one and despise the other. You cannot serve God and money.*
>
> (Luke 16:13 ESV)

The creation of light on the first day confirms what the Apostle Peter taught. We are called to walk in the light as a royal priesthood, and as a holy nation.[5] Peter's words call us out of darkness to minister, serve, and worship as a royal priesthood, a holy nation, and God's special possession. This is a better covenant than Moses pronounced in Exodus, after God, in all His splendor and majesty, brought His chosen people out of slavery in Egypt. God revealed Himself to His people as he separated Israel from their Egyptian captors—light from darkness. Then the Great I AM prepared Israel to become a holy nation set apart to Himself.

> *Then the angel of God, who had been traveling in front of Israel's*
> *army, withdrew and went behind them. The pillar of cloud also*
> *moved from in front and stood behind them, coming between the*
> *armies of Egypt and Israel. Throughout the night the cloud brought*
> *darkness to the one side and light to the other side; so neither went*
> *near the other all night long.*
>
> (Exodus 14:19–20)

In this Scripture, we learn that both light and darkness served God's good purpose: giving light to His people while shrouding their enemy in darkness. Now for us too, God breaks us free from being enslaved to sin's darkness. For those who are set free in Christ, the Scriptures teach us the benefits, beauty, and purpose of walking in the light and choosing to separate ourselves in the light of Christ.

> *I call heaven and earth to witness against you today, that I have set*
> *before you life and death, blessing and curse. Therefore choose life,*
> *that you and your offspring may live.*
>
> (Deuteronomy 30:19 ESV)

> *Or what fellowship has light with darkness?*
>
> (2 Corinthians 6:14 ESV)

> *Once you were not a people, but now you are the people of God; once*
> *you had not received mercy,*
> *but now you have received mercy.*
>
> (1 Peter 2:10 ESV)

---

5. 1 Peter 2:9.

Today we have an advantage that Adam and Eve did not. The deceptive mask of darkness has been exposed and we can see the devastating nature of the dark side. Our eyes are opened to see the light of Christ, and now darkness and light stand in sharp contrast. We must look to the Light of Life and answer His call. We must answer His knock at our heart's door.

Praise him, sun and moon; praise him, all you shining stars. Praise him, you highest heavens and you waters above the skies. Let them praise the name of the Lord, for at his command they were created, and he established them for ever and ever– he issued a decree that will never pass away.

(Psalm 148:3–6)

Now we can see the light of the first day of creation and its purpose in creation. It is light for the heart, Christ the Light of the World, the light of life, light for life's pathway, and light to enlighten God's people. Let's take a closer look at God's great separations to see the beauty and effect of His creation separations.

Rewind, for just a moment, back to the Garden of Eden. The light of the first day is an eternal light. When God placed Adam and Eve in the garden on the sixth day, this light remained to illuminate their hearts. Surely, new songs welled up in their hearts as they pursued the wind of the Spirit flowing through the trees of the garden.

O sing to the Lord a new song; sing to the Lord, all the earth.

(Psalm 96:1).

The wind blows wherever it pleases. You hear its sound, but you cannot tell where it comes from or where it is going.

(John 3:8)

The heavenly Father desired for Adam and Eve to treasure fellowship with Him in their heart of hearts, and to cherish this communion more than the good gifts He poured out with abundance upon His created earth. The light of the first day, for Adam and Eve and for us today, is light to walk in sweet fellowship with our Heavenly Father. The truth revealed in this light is the light of Christ that illuminates the heart.

Light of the knowledge of God's glory displayed in the face of Christ.

(2 Corinthians 4:6)

In this light, we are called out of darkness and separated into the light of Christ so this true and eternal light will illuminate our footsteps all day long and through the night. In the light of the Word of creation, we are separated in Christ. The foundation of this good work was set in place on day one of creation and remains as solid truth for our hearts today.[6]

> *God called the light "day," and the darkness he called "night."*
> *And there was evening, and there was morning–the first day.*
>
> (Genesis 1:5)

Day Two

The Creator continued to separate, creating order out of chaos. He divided the waters of the sky above from the waters for the earth below. In doing this, He set apart water to accomplish His holy purpose. God separated with a clear and distinct purpose as He brought order to the earth.

God's purpose for the waters above and the waters on the earth became evident as He spoke through Moses to the people of His chosen nation. He prophesied rain to pour out from heaven upon the Promised Land rather than the irrigation waters they used in Egypt. He spoke of the refreshing dew of Mount Hermon to cover the land of promise like morning dew; the dew of righteousness.[7]

> *The land you are entering to take over is not like the land of Egypt, from which you have come, where you planted your seed and irrigated it by foot as in a vegetable garden. But the land you are crossing the Jordan to take possession of is a land of mountains and valleys that drinks rain from heaven. It is a land the Lord your God cares for; the eyes of the Lord your God are continually on it from the beginning of the year to its end.*
>
> (Deuteronomy 11:10–12)

Just as Creator God separated the waters above from waters below, He made a clear demarcation between the common waters of Egypt to water their gardens and the dew of heaven for the Land of Promise. Canaan and Egypt are as different as night and day. The land of promise separated them from the land of slavery. The showers upon Israel's portion were showers of righteousness that did not come by the work of man.

---

6. Additional study Scriptures for day one: Job 22:28, Psalm 97:11; 112:4, Proverbs 4:18, Isaiah 58:8; 60:20, John 8:12, 1 John 2:10.
7. Psalm 133:3.

The remnant of Jacob will be in the midst of many peoples like dew from the Lord, like showers on the grass, which do not wait for anyone or depend on man.

(Micah 5:7)

The Creator used water as the base element to create everything else. The Psalmist and Apostle Peter agree on this important point. Water is the Almighty's active ingredient to make everything new.

The earth is the Lord's, and everything in it, the world, and all who live in it; for he founded it on the seas and established it on the waters.

(Psalm 24:1–2)

But they deliberately forget that long ago by God's word the heavens came into being and the earth was formed out of water and by water.

(2 Peter 3:5)

The Spirit of the Lord brooded (incubated) over this earth's egg-shaped, watery, chaotic mass. Out of the earth's primordial chaotic soup, on the second day of creation, God separated water from water—the ocean from the clouds in the sky.

Water was the basis of creation; the means for all that God created. Jesus used spittle to create new eyes for the blind man. We become new creations in Christ in the waters of baptism. In the beginning, God established water with life-sustaining and life-giving power. Water in the hands of a holy God gives life, and sustains life. The dew of Mount Hermon blanketed the Promised Land like the dew of righteousness to prosper the land. The rain watered the soil of the Promised Land to make it a land of "milk and honey" for God's people. The prophet Isaiah proclaimed this truth.

You heavens above, rain down my righteousness; let the clouds shower it down. Let the earth open wide, let salvation spring up, let righteousness flourish with it; I, the Lord, have created it.

(Isaiah 45:8)

Separating the waters on the second day of creation was just the beginning. God separated the waters again to make the tribes of Jacob into a holy nation separated unto Himself.

He divided the sea and led them through; he made the water stand up like a wall. He guided them with the cloud by day and with light from the fire all night. He split the rocks in the wilderness and gave them water as abundant as the seas; he brought streams out of a rocky crag and made water flow down like rivers.

(Psalm 78:13–16)

In the same way that God separated the waters on the second day of creation, He now separates water to serve His holy purpose—waters to cleanse, waters to redeem,[8] water from Jesus' pierced side,[9] waters of holy baptism,[10] waters to accomplish the work of His saving grace.

The Old Testament gives us many illustrations of the cleansing power of water, separated for a holy purpose. The ashes of the red heifer provide an example of this. This young female cow must be without spot or blemish, never have calved, or been under a yoke. Its ashes were added to pure water to prepare what is referred to as waters of separation, to separate God's people for a holy purpose.

A man who is clean shall gather up the ashes of the heifer and put them in a ceremonially clean place outside the camp. They are to be kept by the Israelite community for use in the water of cleansing; it is for purification from sin.

(Numbers 19:9)

Under the Old Covenant, God's people were given a ritual cleansing with water.

But it must also be purified with the water of cleansing. And whatever cannot withstand fire must be put through that water. On the seventh day wash your clothes and you will be clean. Then you may come into the camp.

(Numbers 31:23–24)

Through the waters of the Red Sea, Israel became a unique nation, separated to God.

For I do not want you to be ignorant of the fact, brothers and sisters, that our ancestors were all under the cloud and that they all passed through the sea. They were all baptized into Moses[11] in the cloud and in the sea. They all ate the same spiritual food and drank the same spiritual drink; for they drank from the spiritual rock that accompanied them, and that rock was Christ.

(1 Corinthians 10:1–4)

Again in Noah's day, God used water to separate. The people God created to subdue the earth were instead defiling the earth. But God cleansed the world of wickedness and corruption, and separated Noah and his family from this depravity in the waters of a world-wide flood.[12] The Apostle Peter writes of that day:

---

8. Isaiah 43:1–4.
9. John 19:34.
10. 1 Corinthians 10:2.
11. In this Scripture we see Moses as a type of Christ.
12. Genesis 6.

> *After being made alive, he went and made proclamation to the imprisoned spirits–to those who were disobedient long ago when God waited patiently in the days of Noah while the ark was being built. In it only a few people, eight in all, were saved through water, and this water symbolizes baptism that now saves you also–not the removal of dirt from the body but the pledge of a clear conscience toward God. It saves you by the resurrection of Jesus Christ, who has gone into heaven and is at God's right hand–with angels, authorities and powers in submission to him.*
>
> (1 Peter 3:19–22)

The power and purpose of water in the hands of Almighty God is still at work in us today. In the waters of baptism, we are separated to a holy God.

> *He saved us through the washing of rebirth and renewal by the Holy Spirit, whom he poured out on us generously through Jesus Christ our Savior, so that, having been justified by his grace, we might become heirs having the hope of eternal life.*
>
> (Titus 3:5–7)

What a great hope the Creator holds out to us! Not only the joys of heaven, but forever separated from the chains of sin as we wait for God's promise.

> *Wash away all my iniquity and cleanse me from my sin.*
>
> (Psalm 51:2)

In the following Psalm, we see water in the hands of a holy God to accomplish His purpose of separating His people as His own—a holy nation.

> *When Israel came out of Egypt, Jacob from a people of foreign tongue, Judah became God's sanctuary, Israel his dominion. The sea looked and fled, the Jordan turned back; the mountains leaped like rams, the hills like lambs. Why was it, sea, that you fled? Why, Jordan, did you turn back? Why, mountains, did you leap like rams, you hills, like lambs? Tremble, earth, at the presence of the Lord, at the presence of the God of Jacob, who turned the rock into a pool, the hard rock into springs of water.*
>
> (Psalm 114)

Water is a critical element as we see in the first chapter of Genesis. Fast forward to the last chapter of Revelation where water flows from the throne of God in an ever-expanding river. From beginning to end, God uses water to cleanse, to wash, to separate, to restore, to give new life, and to refresh His people.

It is instructive to see an overview of many references to water separated for God's holy purpose throughout the Scriptures:

- Rescued from the waters of affliction (Psalm 69:15)
- The dew of Mt. Hermon falling upon Zion (Psalm 133:3)
- Waters of salvation (Isaiah 12:3)
- Waters of wrath (Isaiah 54:9)
- A river of healing waters that increases as it flows (Ezekiel 47:3–5)
- Watering the land for God's chosen people (Amos 5:24)
- Sea of glass (Revelation 4:6)
- Springs of Living Water (Revelation 7:17)
- Waters of judgment (Revelation 16:5)
- Water, clear as crystal, flowing from the throne of God (Revelation 22:1)

We become witnesses of the power of God's word and the strength of His mighty arm. He speaks and what He says appears. It is all held together because He is faithful to His word and He remains the same yesterday, today, and forever. Paul wrote to the Colossian church:

He is before all things, and in him all things hold together.

(Colossians 1:17)

Bathed in the Scriptures, we become witnesses of God who created a beautiful earth out of a useless, chaotic, and watery mass. This disorderly sphere was awash in murky water, and covered by the deep. This tumultuous globe was as useless as half a baptism—water without the work of Christ, the Word. In God's good creation, He ordered a house for our habitation. God separated as He began to prepare a bountiful table before us.

Water in the hands of a holy God continues to separate a people as His own—a holy people, a holy nation. This separation begins by faith in water that is separated for a holy purpose—the waters of baptism. In baptismal water we became a new creation in Christ; we are washed and cleansed from every stain of sin. We are bathed to the depths of our being—our conscience cleansed of guilt.

The power and effect of water that God separated for His holy purpose began on day two of creation and continues for us today.

God called the vault "sky."
And there was evening, and there was morning–the second day.

(Genesis 1:8)[13]

---

13. Study Scriptures: Psalm 65:9–10, Job 38:22–23.

Day Three

God separated the dry ground from the waters so the ground could produce vegetation and seed-bearing plants. As we see God's hand at work on this day, once again we witness God establishing order out of chaos. God's created order permeates everything He established among humankind—both what is holy and what is common. Nations, cultures, societies, villages, towns, cities, families, churches, farms, gardens, orchards, and ranches are all set in order with good blessings for all who will inhabit the planet.

As you look at the world around you through this revelatory lens, you will see things in a beautiful light; the light of God who provides—God our Portion.[14] In this light, when you cultivate the soil, plant the seeds, water the garden, or go to your job to provide for your family, you can know that what you are doing is in agreement with God's established order.

God separated the dry land from the waters of the earth. The islands, continents, mountains, and river valleys were separated from the seas. The oceans settled in place as the sands of the shore set a boundary the seas would not cross. Out of the chaotic waters of the earth, God separated dry land for mankind to inhabit. On this dry land God planted seed-bearing plants to grow. Fresh, green grasses would spring up on the dry land and forests grew and flourished. Orchard trees blossomed and provided fruit, and gardens produced food for the people so they would thrive on the earth. All these good things were the fruit of God's creative wisdom. King Solomon, the author of many Proverbs, wrote of wisdom, ever present in creation of the heavens and earth:

I was there when he set the heavens in place, when he marked out the horizon on the face of the deep, when he established the clouds above and fixed securely the fountains of the deep, when he gave the sea its boundary so the waters would not overstep his command, and when he marked out the foundations of the earth. Then I was constantly at his side. I was filled with delight day after day, rejoicing always in his presence, rejoicing in his whole world and delighting in mankind.

(Proverbs 8:27–31)

The wisdom of Proverbs is Christ, the Light of the World. By wisdom He commanded, and the dry land set a boundary for oceans, seas, rivers, and lakes. God's orderly creation, as revealed again on day three of creation, provided dry ground, separated for a purpose. The waters and dry land are for the common good of all mankind, and for the wild animals in the field,

---

14. Psalm 142:5.

forest, and jungle. Dry land would serve as God's open hand of provision for all God's created creatures, and for those created in His image.

All creatures look to you to give them their food at the proper time. When you give it to them they gather it up; when you open your hand, they are satisfied with good things.

(Psalm 104:27–28)

Day three sets the groundwork for the coming days of creation. The dry land is fertile soil to grow abundant fruit for the animals and mankind to gather and enjoy. The waters would provide moisture for the plants to grow and bear fruit.

And there was evening, and there was morning–the third day.

(Genesis 1:13)

Day Four

The Hebrew word used for the light created on the fourth day is מָאוֹר *ma'owr*. The meaning of this is: a luminary. The same word is used for the light from a candlestick. On this day, by His Word, God speaks the luminaries of the sky into being. Christ, the Word, is the voice of creation. He commanded and the light in the skies above the earth came into being.

"Let there be lights in the expanse of the sky to separate the day from the night...and let them be lights in the vault of the sky to give light on the earth." And it was so.

(Genesis 1:14–15)

God separated the day from the night and created the sun, moon, and stars to mark the seasons, days, and years, and to give light on the earth. On the fourth day of creation, we see God reveal Himself as Creator of light for natural eyes. And still today, by His holy presence, God gives light in the night from the moon and stars, and then He drives back the darkness of the night with the first light of the morning sun. This is a light for the common good of all mankind, and for the wild animals that prowl in the jungles and forests. Moses spoke of this natural light of the sun as he prophesied blessings for the tribe of Joseph.

> *Moses said this about the tribes of Joseph: "May their land be blessed by the Lord with the precious gift of dew from the heavens and water from beneath the earth; with the rich fruit that grows in the sun, and the rich harvest produced each month; with the finest crops of the ancient mountains, and the abundance from the everlasting hills; with the best gifts of the earth and its bounty, and the favor of the one who appeared in the burning bush."*
>
> (Deuteronomy 33:13–16 NLT)

The "rich fruit that grows in the sun" includes the common blessings from sunlight that made gardens flourish in a land of milk and honey. This truth is found throughout the Scriptures. The Psalmist wrote of the common light from the sun and moon as luminaries in the sky to govern the day and night.

> *The day is yours, and yours also the night; you established the sun and moon. It was you who set all the boundaries of the earth.*
>
> (Psalm 74:16–17)

Every day, common sunlight also provided for the people living outside the boundaries of Israel's land. Jesus spoke of this common light as He taught the crowds that surrounded Him. In the following verse, Jesus referred to the warmth of sunlight that God sends for all mankind whether they are good or bad.

> *He causes his sun to rise on the evil and the good, and sends rain on the righteous and the unrighteous.*
>
> (Matthew 5:45)

New Testament Greek makes a clearer distinction between common and holy light. Sun for the common good is ἥλιος *hélios*, meaning the sun, rays of the sun, the light of day. This is the light God created on the fourth day of creation. The difference is clear as Jesus also referred to the separating power of the greater eternal light that is φῶς *phōs* when He said:

> *"I am the light of the world. Whoever follows me will not walk in darkness, but will have the light of life."*
>
> (John 8:12 ESV)

The Apostle Paul wrote to the Ephesian church, making reference to the separation of light and darkness. This is the light of the first day of creation.

> *For you were once darkness, but now you are light in the Lord.*
> *Live as children of light (for the fruit of the light consists in all goodness,*
> *righteousness and truth).*
> (Ephesians 5:8–9)

The light in this verse is φῶς *phōs*. This Greek word means: God is light, delicate, subtle, pure, of brilliant quality, the light of truth and knowledge, and spiritual purity. The difference is clear because the light of the fourth day, ἥλιος *hélios*, will cease to shine at the end of time.

> *The sun will no more be your light by day,*
> *nor will the brightness of the moon shine on you,*
> *for the Lord will be your everlasting light, and your God will be your glory.*
> (Isaiah 60:19)

God created the light of the fourth day for the common good. And yet the fourth day's light also serves to direct men's hearts to the light of the first day. The common luminaries serve as God's witnesses in the sky to direct men's hearts to the eternal light of Christ.

> *The heavens declare the glory of God; the skies proclaim the work of his hands.*
> *Day after day they pour forth speech; night after night they reveal knowledge.*
> *They have no speech, they use no words; no sound is heard from them.*
> (Psalm 19:1–3)

The luminaries God created on the fourth day glow out with light for every nation on earth. When a man feels the heat of the sun on his back, or lifts up his eyes to the stars in the heavens, he sees a revelation of God's glory and majesty as Creator of all the heavens and earth. When we observe the sun, moon and stars in the skies above, there is only one possible conclusion: We are compelled to glorify Creator God who formed the heavens and earth by design.

We are warmed in the sunlight of the fourth day of creation. Our gardens grow and flourish in the daylight of the fourth day. Sands on the beach burn our bare feet in the midday sun. We watch as the sun and moon mark the seasons. We yearn for the springtime sunlight to warm the earth and make the flowers bloom. As the sun rises in the morning sky, wild creatures slip out of their burrows to gather food. Nocturnal predators hide in their dens during the heat of the day and come out to hunt in the light of the moon.

We can see that God created this fourth day's sunlight for the common good of mankind and for all of the creatures of the earth. God's created order becomes evident with the words written to finish the day's work:

And God saw that it was good.
And there was evening, and there was morning–the fourth day.

(Genesis 1:18–19)

Day Five

On the first, second, third, and fourth days, God brought order to the earth, making beautifully excellent creations. He separated light from darkness and separated the waters above from the waters below. The Creator brought dry land forth from the waters of the earth. God created seed-bearing plants and vegetation to blanket the earth, and created the sun in the sky to make all creation grow and flourish. Then, after He prepared the earth to support life, God created the living creatures on the fifth day. He created the tiny hummingbirds, and the great condors that fly above. God created the little minnows and the massive blue whales to swim in the sea's currents; each one a beautiful creation to consider. Watching an eagle swoop down and snatch a salmon from the river, enjoying colorful varieties of birds flying through the air, witnessing the antics of orca whales, delighting to see a pod of dolphin leap out of the water, these are the wonders God created on the fifth day—all delights of God's creation. If you love to fish, or if you're a bird watcher, this is one day of creation you're especially thankful for. God spoke into being the birds of the air, and the fish in the sea, from the land and the sea. What a delightful creation He has made for us to enjoy and care for.

The work of creation on the fifth day was in preparation for the sixth day. God would create Adam and Eve on the sixth day and give them instructions about all the creatures He created. Through Adam, the people who would populate the earth were blessed with a charge—a good work to do. They were to care for the earth, protect God's creatures, and enjoy all that God had given for their benefit. It's as if God prepared the joy of fishing. The Creator made working dogs for the duck hunter. The Lord Almighty planted the earth like a garden for people to care for, enjoying God's bounty.

God's praises ought to well up from our souls when we see the beauty He prepared for humankind on the fifth day. God's bounty toward His creation ought to inspire all people to give Him all glory and honor.

For from him and through him and for him are all things.
To him be the glory forever! Amen.

(Romans 11:36)

And there was evening, and there was morning–the fifth day.
(Genesis 1:23)

Day Six

God formed the wild animals out of the ground.[15] The Creator spoke the word, saying; "Let the earth bring forth." He separated creatures from the dust of the earth. And then He also created Adam from the same dust. The Holy Spirit breathed life into Adam and the Lord gave him the job of naming the cattle, the birds, and the wild animals. God brought them before Adam and he gave them each their own name. We can only imagine Adam laughing with delight as he observed the long-necked animals, saying, "You will be called gee-raffe." He must have chuckled when he declared, "My goodness hippo, you have such a big potamus."

On this day, God's created creatures included the domestic animals. They would provide milk for the children, meat for the table, wool for warm clothing, be vigilant to guard property, work for the hunter-gatherer, and serve as companions. God created the horse that thrilled at the pounding of its hooves as he raced through the open fields. God created the elk that bugles in the foothills, the elephant to trumpet on the savannah, and the lion to roar in the wild.

Family also had its beginnings on day six of creation. God separated Adam from the dust of the ground and created Eve from Adam's side, then brought them together for the good work God gave them to do in the garden. He created them for His glory,[16] for fellowship,[17] and to do the good work God prepared for them.[18]

God blessed them and said to them,
"Be fruitful and increase in number; fill the earth and subdue it. Rule over the fish in the sea and the birds in the sky and over every living creature that moves on the ground."
(Genesis 1:28)

We are called to honor the Almighty's orderly creation. This harmonious order ought to be evident in our family life and reflected in all our worship, service, and ministries as disciples of Christ. The Apostle Paul instructs us to worship, minister, and serve in a way that exalts God who created Adam from the dust of the ground and then Eve from Adam's side. The Creator gave woman to stand with the man.[19]

---

15. Genesis 2:19.
16. Isaiah 43:7.
17. 1 Corinthians 1:9.
18. Ephesians 2:10.
19. 1 Corinthians 11:9 CSB. The key word in this verse is "sake." This is the Greek word διά diá, dee-ah': a primary preposition denoting the channel of an act, commonly translated "through" or "on account of."

The science of Yehovah's interdependent, harmonious interworkings of creation is beyond amazing. God created Adam first, and then He formed Eve from Adam. Being alone was not in God's plan. God's orderly creation ought to be reflected as we gather for worship, and in all service and ministries in Jesus name. The harmony of creation should be honored, affect every aspect of our lives, and become evident in our families, churches, communities, in commerce, in our justice system, and in our governments.

God's perfectly ordered creation reveals the Creator as holy. Christ Jesus as head of the church is a perfect model for us. All those who are made in God's image have equal standing in Christ, before God Almighty. This truth ought to be reflected in a Christian's job, community, service, and in caring for the earth. The orderly nature of God's creation must be apparent in our worship gatherings, and in all Christian service and ministries. In all that we do, when we live according to God's created order, the chaos is driven away and everything is brought into order. On the sixth day of creation, God established order within the animal kingdom, and established order for all humankind. This order benefits us in every aspect of our daily lives. On day six of creation, God made all this possible. By His command He brought all these good things into being for our benefit.

> *God saw all that he had made, and it was very good.*
> *And there was evening, and there was morning–the sixth day.*
>
> (Genesis 1:31)

Day Seven

When God completed the work of creation, He separated himself from His labor and entered His rest. This separation is the most beautiful revelation of God's loving, caring nature toward His created beings. God's rest on the seventh day of creation was like crossing a threshold to enter a rest that is eternal, without end. In Christ Jesus and the work of the cross, God provides a way for us to cross this threshold and come into His rest. In fact, He calls each of us by name to come into His rest. A beautiful picture comes to mind of God entering His rest, looking around Him saying, "I am calling Annabelle, Thaddeus, Jason, Omani, Jacob, Nicolás, Masako, Jane, Rayed, Shamone, and all those whose names I have written in the Book of Life to come into my rest."[20] Jesus taught the crowds, and welcomed them into God's rest:

> *Come to me, all you who are weary and burdened, and I will give you rest.*
>
> (Mathew 11:28)

---

20. 2 Thessalonians 2:13.

This day of creation is of greater significance than all the days before because on this day, God established an eternal rest for all who answer His call. God's rest is the icing on the cake, and the sizzle of the steak. This is the "rest" that the writer of Hebrews compels people to enter by faith, and warns them not to refuse.

> *Now we who have believed enter that rest, just as God has said,*
> *"So I declared on oath in my anger, 'They shall never enter my rest.'"*
> *And yet his works have been finished since the creation of the world.*

(Hebrews 4:3)

As God entered His rest on the seventh day, He also desired to separate us from broken hearts, tears, the agony of death, mourning, and from all pain.

> *For all who have entered into God's rest have rested from their labors,*
> *just as God did after creating the world.*

(Hebrews 4:10 NLT)

By faith we enter into God's rest now, and on that final great day we will enter the fullness of God's promised rest. God prepared a seventh day rest to receive us, so we may rest in His presence forever, to serve and worship before the LORD Almighty. To dwell forever with our Heavenly Father will be joy and happiness beyond anything we can imagine. The world's darkness will have passed away, and we will see Him face to face.

> *They will see his face, and his name will be on their foreheads.*
> *There will be no more night. They will not need the light of a lamp or the light of the sun,*
> *for the Lord God will give them light. And they will reign for ever and ever.*

(Revelation 22:4–5)

> *He will wipe every tear from their eyes. There will be no more death or mourning*
> *or crying or pain, for the old order of things has passed away.*

(Revelation 21:4)

This is the beauty, the peace, the comfort, and the immeasurable joy that is ours as we enter God's rest. The Creator prepared this rest for us from the beginning. With loving arms, God reaches out to us. How could we refuse? By faith in Jesus Christ, God's Son, can we enter God's rest today? This is what God has prepared for us as He entered His rest on the seventh day of creation. We can rest assured in this great promise. We have heard God's word, and His promise. By the living power of His word in the Holy Scriptures saving faith may be planted in our heart of hearts.

Will you hear Him calling your name? Will you open the door to faith, believe and receive God's promise of salvation? Talk to God and say what is in your heart. Tell Him what you're struggling with. Talk to Him and say what you believe or desire to believe. Today is the day for you to enter God's rest. By saving grace, by faith, you are delivered from, separated from being caught up in sin's grip. He is ready to break the chains of your sin so that you may cross the threshold and enter His eternal rest.

God's beauty, majesty, and awesome power were made evident in all seven days of creation. The Creator brooded over the chaotic waters of the earth and began separating light from darkness, the waters above from the waters of the earth, day from night, and each day He continued His creation separations until the seventh day when God separated Himself from the work of creation in His rest.

Creations great separations are all reflections of a holy God, for He is holy, holy, holy—the LORD God Almighty. To create by means of separation is consistent with the meaning of holy: to be separate, to be set apart. In all creation we see the glory, majesty, and splendor of God Almighty, Creator of the heavens and earth. In awe of God our knees bow before Him to worship in spirit and truth. To know God compels us to separate ourselves to Christ, who delivers us from the darkness and depravity of the world.

After God brought His creation to order, He continued to separate. Earth's history began with separations and is kept in order by separations. From Noah, Abraham, the patriarchs, and prophets of old, the Lord separated them as they looked forward to Christ. This orderly creation remains to provide an edifice for all the luminaries in the skies above, the seasons of the earth, social structures, family, church, state, and economic systems. We are called to come out and be separate[21] until the end of time.

For all of us who dwell in the earth, we will find the best way to live on the earth is to separate ourselves from the chaos and darkness of this world and live in the light—in accord with God's order that He established during seven days of creation. When we separate ourselves from the disorder and gloom of the world our gatherings for worship, our work, family life, Christian service and ministries, and all governance will be well ordered.

In seven days of separations, God brought order to all His creation. The redemptive power of the cross of Jesus Christ that separates us from the darkness of sin was revealed in the first words of creation. Now, our heavenly Father continues this good work, separating His sons and daughters to Himself. All this serves to show us that we too are called to be separated to Christ

---

21. 2 Corinthians 6:17.

in order to accomplish the work God has given us to do. To finish this Great Commission race we must separate ourselves from attempting the final leg of the race in the strength of our common talents and abilities. We must count as nothing our stellar résumés, our list of accomplishments, our degrees, and certifications, because they are insufficient for the challenge ahead. The work before us is impossible on our own, and we do not have what it takes to reach the finish line. The strength needed in our time to accomplish this great task can only come by means of the anointing, gifting, and empowering work of the Spirit of Jesus Christ.

Let what is common serve God's good purpose to provide for us and for our families here on earth. But now is the time to be separated to accomplish the work of the Great Commission by means of the power of the Spirit of God, who is holy.

Chapter 2
The Word of Creation
Q & A

1. Describe the light of the first day of creation. How is it different from the light on the fourth day of creation?

   _____

   _____

   _____

2. With each new day, the Creator brought about a greater harmony. What does this reveal to you about God's nature?

   _____

   _____

   _____

3. Why is it important to understand that God is sovereign over all, even over darkness?

   _____

   _____

   _____

4. Try to imagine the joy of naming all the animals. What would you have called the giraffe?

   _____

   _____

   _____

My Journal Notes:

Chapter 3:
Great Separation Sequels

Key Scriptures:

- "Although the whole earth is mine, you will be for me a kingdom of priests and a holy nation." (Exodus 19:5–6)
- "Paul, a bondservant of Jesus Christ, called to be an apostle, separated to the gospel of God." (Romans 1:1 NKJV)

God's great separations on the first seven days of creation were an awesome beginning. But the Creator did not set the world in order like a wind-up toy, only to let it dawdle along its way through the ages. God actively continues to separate throughout all time, as if in sequels. The Almighty continues separating because He is holy. God separated Adam and Eve from the Garden of Eden because of their sin. The LORD separated Cain—banished him because of the darkness that ruled his heart. Almighty God separated Noah to redeem him from the corruption and evil that surrounded him on an earth defiled by the sins of humankind. Abram and Sarai were separated from family and homeland to go to a land God would show them. Jehovah God separated Joseph from his family to fulfill God's purpose of saving his kin from famine so Israel would become a holy nation. Jesus was Light in a land of darkness, and the power of His resurrection proclaimed light to all people.[1] The LORD sent the Apostle Paul to turn people's hearts from darkness to light.[2]

We find many means for separating in the Bible: the sword, the Living Stone, waters of separation, refining fire, the Good Shepherd's staff, and the cleansing blood of the Lamb. God, in His perfect love, separates His people from evil and corruption in the world that would destroy them. He brings them into His sanctuary; into His protection, peace, comfort, joy, strength, and rest. Indeed, the Almighty has assigned a time of reckoning to uphold this great cause.[3] The final episode in this series of separations is when the Son of Man comes in His glory with His Shepherd's staff in hand to forever separate "sheep from goats."

The evil and darkness of the world surrounds God's people, trying to defeat us. The chains of sin attempt to keep us from the fullness of Christ. When we are caught up in sin's shackles, we long to be separated from—freed from this oppression. Being bound in sin steals away sweet fellowship with a loving, caring, compassionate Heavenly Father. But from this bondage we can cry

---
1. Isaiah 9:2, Acts 26:23.
2. Acts 26:18.
3. Isaiah 34:8.

out to God who hears us, and He will deliver us and separate us. This deliverance and freedom are the work of Jesus' double-edged sword. Jesus Christ is also the stone that separates. The power of the blood of Jesus Christ, blood He shed on a cruel Roman cross, cleanses us of the stain of sin. The Spirit of Jesus is the fire that separates and refines. Purification is given us in the waters of separation[4]—our baptism. Each and every means of separation is given to us in Christ to empower us for the work before us and for our eternal benefit.

The Sword that Separates

The Scriptures reveal a beautiful truth about the work of the sword. God's only Son is the Word of creation, ever present as God created all the heavens and earth. As Jesus walked among us, he continued the work of separating. He declared:

"I did not come to bring peace, but a sword."

(Matthew 10:34)

What was Jesus saying? The book of Hebrews sheds light on this truth, and we learn that the sword is for dividing and separating.

For the word of God is alive and active. Sharper than any double-edged sword, it penetrates even to dividing soul and spirit, joints and marrow; it judges the thoughts and attitudes of the heart.

(Hebrews 4:12)

This is the sword He brought—the Word of God that separates, like separating bone from marrow, wheat from chaff, sheep from goats, light from darkness. This double-edged sword is sharp enough to divide soul and spirit, which is as difficult as separating bone from marrow.

For those who are in Christ, the sword that separates is a great help and comfort. For those who oppose Christ, His double-edged sword is to be feared. Like King Solomon's sword,[5] this is the sword that separates, revealing truth and exposing a lie. By means of His word, Christ separates us from the darkness of deceit to bring us into the light of truth. God does this because we cannot serve both light and darkness. We cannot be both a bondservant of the God of Light and a slave to darkness.[6]

---

4. Numbers 19:9.
5. 1 Kings 3:16–28.
6. 2 Corinthians 6:14.

The Living Stone that Separates

The Apostle Peter wrote to the churches about the living Stone that separates—Jesus Christ. For those who answer Jesus' call, the Stone is precious. For those who reject the Cornerstone, it causes them to stumble.[7] It becomes the Rock that causes them fall. This precious Stone sets apart in Christ. Those who receive the gift of saving faith and those who reject the message of the Gospel are set apart. For those who refuse Christ, the living Stone rightfully trips them up. The Cornerstone separates the rebellious from those who will worship, serve and minister as living stones before God as a royal priesthood. The work of the living Stone is revealed in the following Scripture:

As you come to him, the living Stone–rejected by humans but chosen by God and precious to him–you also, like living stones, are being built into a spiritual house to be a holy priesthood, offering spiritual sacrifices acceptable to God through Jesus Christ.
For in Scripture it says:
"See, I lay a stone in Zion, a chosen and precious cornerstone,
and the one who trusts in him will never be put to shame."
Now to you who believe, this stone is precious.
But to those who do not believe,
"The stone the builders rejected has become the cornerstone," and,
"A stone that causes people to stumble and a rock that makes them fall."
They stumble because they disobey the message–which is also what they were destined for.
But you are a chosen people, a royal priesthood, a holy nation, God's special possession, that you may declare the praises of him who called you out of darkness into his wonderful light. Once you were not a people, but now you are the people of God; once you had not received mercy, but now you have received mercy.

(1 Peter 2:4–10)

A beautiful picture of Christ the living Stone is found in the story about King Saul's obsessive pursuit of David, God's anointed. David and his band of fugitives rushed along on one side of the mountain and King Saul and his army charged on in hot pursuit on the other side of the mountain. But then Saul received an urgent message about a foreign army attacking Israel and he turned his army around to go fight the invaders. The rock that separated Saul from David was thereafter called the Rock of Escape, or the Rock of Separation.[8]

---

7. Matthew 21:41–44, Psalm 118:20–24.
8. 1 Samuel 23:28.

The Rock that separated King Saul and David is with us today. He is Jesus Christ the Stone who is living and actively present to deliver us from the chains of our own sins so we may minister, serve, and worship as a royal priesthood without fear; in holiness and righteousness before God Almighty all our days.[9]

Waters of Separation

Water is the most abundant element on earth. Wetlands, streams, rivers, lakes, seas, and oceans make up most of the earth's surface. The human body is about sixty percent water. Cool water quenches our thirst and refreshes us during a long, hot summer day. The rain refreshes the earth's vegetation and makes it fruitful. Abundant water is one of God's many common blessings for the good of humankind, field, forest, and animals alike.

The Great I AM has demonstrated many more profound uses for water. In Noah's day, the waters of the deep and waters above flooded the whole world to cleanse it of the depravity that corrupted the earth. But God sealed Noah and the animals in the ark, separating them from the destruction of the earth below. Pharaoh's daughter rescued baby Moses from a basket floating in the water, and this separated him from the ruler's edict that all Hebrew boys be drowned in the Nile. Through the waters of the Red Sea, Yehovah God rescued the tribes of Israel, and then crushed the horses and chariots of Pharaoh's army as the walls of water rushed back. The Lord Yehovah held back the waters of the Jordan River so the Israelites could cross over on dry land.

Another example of the power of God's word and water is found in the muddy waters of the Jordan River. The Syrian army commander, Naaman, dipped himself seven times in the murky water, just as the Prophet Elisha told him, to heal his skin of leprosy. By the power of God's word, water is set aside for a holy purpose, according to God's plan.

Water set apart to accomplish the work of the kingdom of heaven is no longer common. When water is separated by God's word, by His command, it is holy. For us today, God's children are miraculously brought out of the darkness of sin and joined with Christ by the washing of water with the word. By means of water, and in water, the sin that separated us from our Heavenly Father is washed away. In the holy waters of baptism, we are freed from the chains of sin and made one with Christ. We are brought into a family of fellowship. Baptismal waters separate us from the darkness of the world to make us presentable before God in the righteousness of Christ—a clean and radiant church.

---

9. Luke 1:74.

By the power of water together with the Word, all who come to saving faith are separated to Christ. This separation by water and the Word is for the redemption of a lost soul, and is the greatest of all miracles that God has done by means of water that is set apart for a holy purpose.

Fire that Separates

God's holy fire serves to purify and refine, in the process of separating us to Christ. The Spirit's fire refines us like dross separated from silver. This is fire that cleanses, like a needle being disinfected before removing a splinter. The LORD's fire is a consuming fire, like a fire to burn away a field's old stubble to make way for a new crop to grow. This is fire that "tests our mettle" so to speak. When we are refined, cleaned up, have old stuff burned away, and tested, it is stressful and painful in the moment, but the benefits are eternal.

We see an example of this fire at work as the great I AM prepared Moses to lead his people out of slavery in Egypt. God appeared to Moses in the fire of a burning bush.[10] The bush blazed as God spoke to Moses, but the fire did not burn it up. Again, as Moses led the tribes of Israel out of Egypt, pillars of clouds and fire came between the freed slaves and the Egyptian army.[11] God used fire again when the prophet Elijah and Elisha were separated as a chariot and horses of fire brought Elijah to heaven in a whirlwind.[12]

Fire in the hands of an awesome God is a refining fire. In Revelation 3:18, we are counseled to buy from heaven's treasures, gold refined in fires of glory. This gold refined in fire makes us spiritually rich. The prophet Zechariah spoke what he heard God, saying,

> *I will refine them like silver and test them like gold.*
>
> (Zechariah 13:9)

God's refining work in Israel would lead them to call upon Him and He would answer by calling them "my people." Like the people of old, the fires of affliction prove the genuineness of our faith, which is so much greater than earth's gold, even after being refined in a smelter's fire. The purpose of this fire is to separate the dross from precious metal, and the result is praise, glory, and honor for Christ who is revealed.[13] Isaiah teaches us about the refiner's fire, speaking what he heard God saying:

> *I have tested you in the furnace of affliction.*
>
> (Isaiah 48:10)

---

10. Exodus 3:2.
11. Exodus 13:21–22.
12. 2 Kings 2:11.
13. 1 Peter 1:7.

The writer of Proverbs speaks of this refining fire as "testing the heart."[14] One Old Testament account warns of the serious nature of not distinguishing what is holy from what is common.

Aaron's sons Nadab and Abihu took the temple's censers, put fire in them and added incense; and offered unauthorized fire before the Lord, contrary to God's command. So fire came out from the presence of the Lord and consumed them, and they died before the Lord. Moses then said to Aaron, "This is what the Lord spoke of when he said:
'Among those who approach me I will be proved holy;
in the sight of all the people I will be honored.'"

(Leviticus 10:1–3)

What happened to Nadab and Abihu is an example for us, to teach us the reality of God's holiness. This teaches us that we are called to serve, worship, and minister before a holy God by means of the anointing, gifting, and empowering of the Spirit of Jesus Christ. This is a vital part of what John the Baptizer prophesied:

He will baptize you with the Holy Spirit and fire.

(Matthew 3:11)

When we serve, worship, and minister, we are called to separate ourselves from doing so by means of human strength and common gifts and talents. Indeed, to be consumed by the fire of the LORD like Nadab and Abihu is fearful to think about. But fear not! We can learn from their errors. When we serve in holy fear of the LORD,[15] and minister by means of His power and might, there is no need for slave-like fear. When we separate ourselves to serve by means of the fire of the Spirit, we need not fear anything the world throws at us.

The Good Shepherd's Staff that Separates

A shepherd's staff provided great comfort for a playful lamb. A lamb could frolic and play, search for fresh grass garnished with drops of morning dew, while knowing that the shepherd, with rod in hand, watched over him. The shepherd's rod would be quick to strike down a predator, guide the lamb to better pasture, and always ready to pull him out when tangled in a thorn bush. The shepherd used a rod to check every sheep to see if they needed treatment with healing oils. He used his staff to separate the sheep from the goats. At the end of the day the shepherd used the rod to count the sheep to be sure none were missing. The flock found comfort knowing the shepherd and his staff were there to care for them. These word pictures are given to

---
14. Proverbs 17:3.
15. Fear of the Lord is defined as: reverence, awe, and delighted obedience.

teach us so that we may be comforted. We are indeed, the sheep of God's pasture.

> *Know that the Lord is God. It is he who made us, and we are his;*
> *we are his people, the sheep of his pasture.*
>
> (Psalm 100:3)

The shepherd's rod illustrates that God has established a standard to examine the sheep of His pasture. By this measure, a shepherd can know if a sheep needs to be anointed with the healing oil of God's word.[16] When counted among the "sheep of God's pasture," it's a great comfort to know you have been called by name as one of His own. It's heartening to know you have been brought into God's promise.

> *I will take note of you as you pass under my rod,*
> *and I will bring you into the bond of the covenant.*
>
> (Ezekiel 20:37)

In the darkest moments of life, when everything seems to be crashing in upon us, the Good Shepherd's rod protects and provides. We have no need to fear when we feel threatened by the hungry roars of a prowling lion.

> *Even though I walk through the darkest valley, I will fear no evil, for you are with me;*
> *your rod and your staff, they comfort me.*
>
> (Psalm 23:4)

We are blessed with an overwhelming abundance of comfort provided by the Good Shepherd's staff. He uses this rod to count us as His own, to keep us from sickness, to keep us from danger, to guide us to abundant provisions, and to separate us from the goats! What joy, what comfort to be separated into the promise of Christ Jesus, our LORD and Savior. This is a separation with a great and eternal purpose.

The Cross of Jesus Christ that Separates

The way of the cross is the way of peace. Jesus' blood shed on the cross destroyed the barriers to make peace that reconciles us to God. Through Jesus' suffering on the cross, we are made one with Christ in His affliction and death for a good purpose—to bring us together with Christ in His glory. By the work of the cross, we are freed from the Law that condemned us to death, and we are made right with God. Our debt is paid in full and we are separated from the death penalty of sin and joined together with Christ in life and

---
16. Psalm 23:5.

righteousness. We were far away from God, bound in the chains of sin; but by the work of the cross of Jesus Christ we are brought into close fellowship with the Father. When crucified with Christ, in the waters of baptism, we are separated from the world and it no longer holds any power over us.

We were once separated from God, enemies of Christ because of the chains of sin that bound us, but we are brought into right relationship with God through the cross of Christ Jesus.

> *But now he has reconciled you by Christ's physical body through death to present you holy in his sight, without blemish and free from accusation.*
>
> (Colossians 1:22)

No longer ruined by sin, and no longer accused, we may come to dwell in the fullness of Christ, for by the cross Jesus has declared victory over death and darkness. Our human weaknesses no longer rule over us, because the cross separates us from their power. It is by means of the cross that baptism joins us together with Christ; in His suffering, death, and burial, and in His resurrection. We are now alive in Christ: forgiven, cleansed, and no longer under the curse of death. All the shackles that bound us were nailed to the cross—they have no power over us. We are no longer defeated, but at peace with Creator God—triumphant by means of the cross of Jesus Christ.[17] We are separated for a great and eternal purpose.

Forgiveness that Separates

The vital nature of forgiveness is illustrated by the crowds who came to Jesus to be healed. So often, in these moments, Jesus would begin by forgiving their sins. He didn't accuse them of sin, but forgave the sin. Then, with the burden of sin lifted; Jesus touched them, and spoke healing to them. He restored their souls and their health like a one-two punch. He healed their sinful condition, and the heaviness of physical sickness with a double remedy that began with forgiveness.[18]

Forgiveness lifts the burden of sin, cleans away the stain of our sin, and brings us to God's rest. In the same way, we are admonished to forgive, as we have been forgiven, so those around us may share in the same benefits. To forgive brings an end to bitterness, rage, anger, fighting, slander, and malicious talk, making room for kindness and compassion to hold sway.

When sins hold us captive like a ball and chain, when we're like a walking death; the forgiveness of Christ Jesus leads us to die to our old ways that have

---
17. See Galatians 6, Ephesians 2, Colossians 1–2.
18. Matthew 11:28.

trapped us. We become a new creation—alive in Christ. Should we do any less for anyone who has harmed or offended us? By means of forgiveness, we are called to free the one who harmed us from the weight of their offence. When we do forgive, we will be forgiven in the same way.

> *And when you stand praying, if you hold anything against anyone, forgive them,*
> *so that your Father in heaven may forgive you your sins.*
>
> (Mark 11:25)

When you forgive others, you are separated from a sorrowful burden. Your forgiveness of others prepares you so that your heavenly Father will forgive you in like manner. But to forgive from the heart is an impossible human act. Only in Christ is this great separation possible that comes through forgiveness. You will find a great sense of comfort and freedom when Christ Jesus sets you free from the weight of your sin, and cleanses you of its stain. You will also have a great burden lifted from your shoulders when you forgive those who have hurt and offended you. This is a reality because in forgiveness you are delivered from doubt and reaffirmed in your faith.[19] In forgiveness you are separated from the darkness of sin, and brought into the light of Christ for a great and eternal purpose.

The Final Separation

Every moment of time was clear to Creator God as He brought forth the first light of creation. From day one when He separated light from darkness, the LORD God could see Adam's fall and every moment to the end of time. On the first day of creation, God's final victory over sin and death became real, when the darkness would be gone forever and ever. With the darkness gone, the Creator saw no more death, mourning, crying, or pain. Those who are in Christ will be forever separated from the world's chaos and darkness. The Spirit of Jesus spoke this truth to the Apostle John, saying:

> *"I am the Alpha and the Omega," says the Lord God,*
> *"who is, and who was, and who is to come, the Almighty."*
>
> (Revelation 1:8)

Jesus told many parables about the final victorious separation in the kingdom of heaven. He likened the kingdom to weeds and wheat being separated during harvest—the weeds to be burned and the wheat gathered and threshed. Jesus taught that the end of the age would be like when fish are caught in a net. The good fish will be gathered in baskets and the bad thrown away. In the same way the wicked will be separated from the righteous.

19. Study Scriptures: Matthew 11, 2 Corinthians 2, Ephesians 4, and Colossians 2..

Again, Jesus taught His disciples about when the Son of Man comes in His glory, He will separate people like a shepherd separates sheep from goats. He will establish a great chasm that cannot be crossed to separate those who are called by His holy name. Jesus foretold His return, telling what it will be like. There will be two people in bed, one left sleeping and another gathered to His kingdom; one left at the grinding wheel, and the other taken away.

We can let out a great sigh of relief to know we will finally be separated from death, sorrow, weeping, sickness, and all the darkness of the world. We will spend an eternity living in God's eternal light where there will be no more tears.[20] This is God's great and eternal purpose.

When you pass through the waters, I will be with you; and when you pass through the rivers, they will not sweep over you. When you walk through the fire, you will not be burned; the flames will not set you ablaze.

(Isaiah 43:2)

Isaiah's power-packed verse embodies God's amazing acts that began with separating light from darkness. The Almighty continues this good work separating His children out of troubled waters, as if continuing His good work in sequels. His words resonate with each of us because we have all passed through or been dragged through life's turbulent waters. We have all experienced life's tumult that roils us like class five rapids. The prophet's words apply to life in today's corporate jungle, and yet at the root of his prophetic words is hope and deliverance. "When you pass through the waters" is a direct reference to the twelve tribes passing through the waters of the Red Sea. "When you pass through the rivers" made reference to the people crossing over the Jordan River into the Promised Land. "When you walk through the fire" speaks of Israel marching around Jericho for seven days until the angels of the Lord made the walls crumble. Then they burned and destroyed the city. These are the flames God's people passed through as their wandering years ended and they were made a holy nation—separated to Jehovah God the Great I AM.

Crossing the Red Sea, walking over the Jordon's River bed, and entering the Promised Land through the fires of Jericho all serve as illustrations to teach us today. We are also separated by means of water and fire. In the waters of baptism, we are separated from slavery to sin and made one in Christ. We are brought into God's family and given a new name. We pass through the rivers as we continue to live in our baptism and walk as Jesus walked. As prophesied by John the Baptizer, Jesus baptizes in fire. This is the fire of the

---

20. Study Scriptures: Matthew 13; 25, Luke 16–17.

Spirit that sanctifies, anoints, gifts, and empowers you to do the work of the kingdom of heaven. Indeed, the kingdom of heaven is your Promised Land.

God is holy, and because He is holy, it's His very nature to separate. God began by making great separations to create a new earth from a chaotic mass. The Creator separated light from darkness, the waters above from the waters below. But then the Creator continues to separate like many blockbuster sequels to an awesome show. The mighty sword that separates is God's holy word that reveals truth and exposes lies. The Living Stone separates by causing those in rebellion to stumble, and as a foundation for those who serve, worship, and minister as a royal priesthood before a holy God. By the washing of water in holy baptism, we enter into Christ in His death and made new creations in Christ and part of the body of Christ. The baptizing fire of the Spirit of Jesus cleanses, purifies, and empowers God's people to do the work of the church, the kingdom of heaven and the Great Commission. We serve as the Almighty's hands, feet, and mouthpiece in the work of the kingdom of heaven, playing our role in heaven's separating sequels.

As sheep in God's pasture, we are comforted because the Good Shepherd's staff is used to count us as His own—separating the sheep from the goats. We are comforted in His protection, provision, healing, and guidance. On a cruel Roman cross, our Lord Jesus was crucified so that we may be separated from death and made alive in Christ. Jesus' death and resurrection separates us from being defeated in sin to being triumphant in Christ. In forgiveness, we are separated from the darkness and burden of sin and restored in the light of Christ. God has prepared a great final separation for His children. We will be eternally separated from all death, sorrow, weeping, and sickness; to dwell with our heavenly Father in His eternal light.

God created the heavens and the earth by means of separating—because He is holy. The Lord Almighty continued to separate throughout history through His servants Noah, Abraham, Sarah, Moses, Joshua, David, Daniel, Mary, and so many other heroes of our faith. The victory of the cross of Jesus Christ separates us from death and brings to us eternal life. And God has prepared a great and final separation where we will dwell with Him for all eternity.

God's great separations teach us that to serve, minister, and worship before a holy God with great effect we must be like the heroes of our faith, who were called to separate themselves to the Lord. They considered their human strengths and abilities as nothing; even as a loss. This separation is like getting a second wind to run the Great Commission race to the finish line. There is great strength in separating ourselves in Christ, and receiving His Spirit's anointing, gifting, and power so we may accomplish an otherwise impossible work that is ordained for us in our day.

Isaac Watts proclaimed this truth when he wrote this great hymn of the church:

> *"When I survey the wond'rous cross,*
> *On which the Prince of Glory dy'd.*
> *My richest Gain I count but Loss,*
> *And pour Contempt on all my Pride."*

Chapter 3
Great Separation Sequels
Q & A

1. What is God's good purpose in all the separations He has accomplished throughout time?
   _____
   _____
   _____

2. Describe the elements that God uses to separate.
   _____
   _____
   _____

3. What is the power and effect of the waters of baptism?
   _____
   _____
   _____

4. What do the heroes of our faith teach us about God's separations?
   _____
   _____
   _____

My Journal Notes:

Chapter 4:
The Pathway of Light

Key Scriptures:

- "When Aaron and all the Israelites saw Moses, his face was radiant, and they were afraid to come near him." (Exodus 34:30)
- "There he was transfigured before them. His face shone like the sun, and his clothes became as white as the light." (Matthew 17:2)

The light shining from Moses' face as he descended from God's presence on Mount Sinai was the light of the first day of creation. The light that encompassed and radiated from Jesus on the Mount of Transfiguration was the light revealed on earth's first day. This light is greater than the common luminaries in the sky God created on the fourth day, which is natural light from the sun, moon, and stars. The light God separated from darkness on day one enlightens the earth to reveal a holy God. Keep in mind that the meaning of this Hebrew word for "light," אוֹר *'owr*,[1] is light that affects righteousness, prosperity, goodness, and truth. This light of Righteousness is the scepter of the throne for our LORD, Jesus Christ.[2] This is the light God separated out of darkness.[3] This is the light God calls us into as He separates us from darkness.[4]

Take time to pray, read, and meditate on the coming Scriptures to enjoy the full fruit of the message. Then look forward to seeing the righteous effect take hold in your life. The objective for this chapter is to show the purpose and effect of the first day's light in contrast with the fourth day's light. When we see God's purpose for each light, we will be able to separate what is holy from what is common.

Take some time to write on your journal page what the Spirit of Jesus reveals to you about the miraculous light God created on the first day. The fourth day's light, in contrast, was given for the common good of all humankind. It's important to understand God's purpose for both the first and fourth day's light. The light of the first day is for all those who are in Christ—called to do the work of the church, the kingdom of heaven, and the Great Commission. The work of the kingdom is accomplished in the power of the first day's light. It's as if the first day's light is a spiritual vitamin to strengthen the spirit, while the fourth day's light is vitamin D for your body.

---

1. The light of the fourth day is מָאוֹר *ma'owr*, luminaries in the sky above.
2. Hebrews 1:8.
3. Isaiah 58:8.
4. Here, light is used in the same sense as; Job 22:28; 30:26, Psalm 97:11, Proverbs 6:23, Isaiah 9:1; 10:17; 49:6; 51:4, 60:1–3.

It's important to have a clear understanding of this principle, because as we approach the finish line we need the gifting and empowering work of the Spirit of Jesus to give us the "wind" we need for the final sprint of the Great Commission. We also need God's common blessings to sustain our lives and provide for our families. Each light is excellent for its intended purpose.

For you were once darkness, but now you are light in the Lord. Live as children of light (for the fruit of the light consists in all goodness, righteousness and truth) and find out what pleases the Lord. Have nothing to do with the fruitless deeds of darkness, but rather expose them. It is shameful even to mention what the disobedient do in secret. But everything exposed by the light becomes visible–and everything that is illuminated becomes a light. This is why it is said: "Wake up, sleeper, rise from the dead, and Christ will shine on you."

(Ephesians 5:8–14)

But the path of the righteous is like the light of dawn, which shines brighter and brighter until full day.

(Proverbs 4:18 ESV)

He will bring forth your righteousness as the light, and your judgment as the noonday.

(Psalm 37:6 ESV)

For God, who said, "Let light shine out of darkness," made his light shine in our hearts to give us the light of the knowledge of God's glory displayed in the face of Christ.

(2 Corinthians 4:6)

Every good and perfect gift is from above, coming down from the Father of the heavenly lights, who does not change like shifting shadows.

(James 1:17)

The light described in the above Scriptures is the light of holiness, of life; the light of resurrection power, the light of revelation, a light to cleanse, the light of renewal, a light that beckons us, and an ever-brightening light. This light will enlighten our pathway, keep us from stumbling, instruct our mind, and it will burn the darkness out of the deepest recesses of our heart. There is so much to explore regarding the purpose and effect of this eternal light. The life of shepherd boy David who became the Shepherd of Israel illustrates for us how God's great light shines out from the least of us.

Strengthened in the Light

> *Blessed are those whose strength is in you, whose hearts are set on pilgrimage.*
> *As they pass through the Valley of Baka, they make it a place of springs;*
> *the autumn rains also cover it with pools.*
>
> (Psalm 84:5–6)

In every sense, this verse foretells the condition of the Christian Church today. The key phrase is "those whose strength is in you," for these words are the key to understanding our great weakness in the modern church. Too often we depend upon studied interpretations of Hebrew and Greek words. These things have their place, but we must find our strength in the power of the Spirit of Jesus. We rely upon our excellent theological training to give us the tools for the work of ministry and no longer call on the Holy Spirit to interpret Scripture. Classes and seminars teach good business and organizational skills to strengthen our church administrations, service ministries, and charitable organizations. But too often we overlook the power of Christ as the Head of the church. Christians too often rely upon degrees, certificates, and proven management tools to strengthen the church. But we diminish the means Christ has given to empower His church when we are self-reliant. We use worldly attractions to bring people into our church where we celebrate a hipster-style Jesus, because we do not separate what is holy from what is common. A definition of the Hebrew word for holy will show the significance of God's separations. The word "holy" is: קָדוֹשׁ *qâdash*: to consecrate, sanctify, be holy, be hallowed, be separate. Indeed, what is consecrated, sanctified, and hallowed must be separated to be holy.

In too many churches, our Elders are reduced to corporate board members, policy administrators, business supervisors, financial managers, facility directors, and publishers of the church calendar. The vision for the church is a master plan put together by a committee, rather than fasting and a prayerful search for the LORD's purpose and plan.

Even more than this, we have tuned our ears to motivational messages shouted out from every quarter. These voices teach us, "You can chase a lion." Inspirational speakers encourage us, saying, "Pursue your dream and become all you can be." The self-promoters call out, "Live your dream." The flatterer says, "You can do anything you set your heart to do."

But the spiritual battles we fight and the work we set our hearts to do are the ministries and service of the kingdom of light. It's the work of an unseen, eternal realm. The business of commerce in the great corporate jungle is a different battle with its own market-appropriate methods. But the spiritual battles we fight are not fought on terra firma.

For our struggle is not against flesh and blood, but against the rulers, against the authorities, against the powers of this dark world and against the spiritual forces of evil in the heavenly realms.

(Ephesians 6:12)

There's something amiss in all the chattering messages and methodology. One must wonder if we hear what motivational speakers teach. We must ask ourselves, "Do their words hold true when held to the standard of God's word? Is the work of the church accomplished by motivational inspiration, strategic plans, and focus groups alone?"

God's word calls us out of this chaos to make the way straight by the power of the Spirit of Jesus. The Holy Scriptures bring us into reality by comparing us to sheep when it would be more positive and motivating to say we are like lions. Maybe it's because we *are* like sheep. Yes, we are the sheep of His pasture,[5] and our LORD Jesus is the Lion of Judah.[6] He is strong and mighty, and we are like defenseless sheep. Yet this sheep-like state of being is not weak-kneed and hopeless because He is our Good Shepherd and His rod and staff guide and comfort us.[7]

Even more than this, the Lion of Judah indwells us—not to make us mighty sheep, but to manifest the power and might of the Lion of Judah in the most unlikely of His creation. Those who see us will not look and say; "Wow, that sheep is as strong as a lion." No; they will see that the Lion of Judah is mighty in us and through us, doing what we as sheep could never do on our own, and all for the glory of God Almighty.

It may help to look at it like this: When a bear stalks a herd of sheep, what would happen if one of the sheep decided to rise up, dream big, be strong, and take on the predator? With boldness, the sheep would stare into the bear's eyes and charge with all its might, its head down, running faster than he has ever run before. What would happen? The bear could just lie down, yawn, and take the sheep down with one quick bite. The sheep of God's pasture cannot, in their greatest moment of strength, take on the ravenous lion. The Apostle Peter warns us:

Be alert and of sober mind. Your enemy the devil prowls around like a roaring lion looking for someone to devour.

(1 Peter 5:8)

---
5. Psalm 100:3.
6. Revelation 5:5.
7. Psalm 23:4.

In the light of Christ Jesus, we are given the greatest hope. He is the Lion of Judah. He is greater than any bear or lion that may attack. Our Good Shepherd is the Lion who will defeat the predators that would devour us. The same truth about protection in the light of Christ reveals to us that God will use weak sheep as His instruments to do His work in His strength. In this, God is glorified. All who see what God's sheep accomplish by means of the light of Christ in them will give glory to God Almighty because they know that no sheep could achieve such a thing on their own.

The point is worth repeating for emphasis. Much of the modern-day church has lost its eternal perspective. Our vision is blurred if we think of Eleazar, one of David's mighty warriors,[8] as taking the offensive with an adrenaline surge to attack with his sword in hand and defeat a whole enemy army. If we think that David killed Goliath in an adrenaline rush, we're rowing the wrong boat the wrong way up the wrong stream. Those who believe that these men rose up in a sudden surge of human strength are fighting with the wrong weapons.

David's mighty men did not rise up to be the best they could be. They didn't have a blast of human strength that made them superheroes. No! They were like the black sheep in God's pasture. They were the weakest, despised and discounted as misfits, dropouts, and failures. They were tax evaders, the downtrodden of society, and fugitives from debtor's enslavement. These broken men were running from the law. But they submitted in their human weakness to a holy God whose Spirit came upon them to fight the battle. They were weak, but willing sheep. Because of this, Eleazar manifested God's power as a warrior as he struck down an overwhelming enemy with only his sword in hand.

God manifested His power in shepherd boy David when he faced a giant with a slingshot and stone. It was obvious to everyone that the battle was *not* won by human might, power or prowess, and God received all the glory. The LORD fought this battle; the victory belonged to God, and all glory to God Almighty.

If you've ever stepped foot in Sunday school as a child, you've heard the account of David and Goliath.[9] To get to the truth of this story, it is important to separate what is holy from what is common. How could a young shepherd boy kill a nine-foot-tall giant who carried a 125-pound spear, with a shield bearer to protect him? Was it because he practiced and became skilled with his slingshot? Or did David slay the lions and bears that came to steal

---

8. 2 Samuel 23.
9. 1 Samuel 17.

his sheep, and then kill Goliath because of the power of the Spirit at work through him? We're quick to give the Sunday school answer: "by the power of the Spirit." But when we apply the principles of this story to our lives, too often we live out a belief that physical strength and practiced skill won the battle.

We live in a time when the sheep of God's pasture must be anointed, gifted and empowered in the Spirit of Jesus to complete the work of the Great Commission. This great work cannot be accomplished by common means—by human strength alone. We must separate what is common from what is holy to have strength for an eternal task. Today is the time for a great separation that is only possible in the light of Christ

God's Light Shines Brightest in Weak Vessels

Let's explore David's life in greater depth to see that God's power is best manifested in people the world sees as faint, fragile, or of little value. When we read King David's story in the Bible, this truth becomes clear. He was the least regarded of his brothers, the youngest child—the runt of the litter, so to speak. His brothers were burly warriors who put David in his place as a shepherd boy of the family's few sheep. They considered him useful only as a sheepherder out in the wilderness with the stinking, flea-infested flocks. But the Spirit of a holy God came upon him for a good purpose.

No doubt, David practiced and practiced to become skillful in the use of his sling. Most likely he was gifted *and* prepared, having excellent hand-eye coordination. This talent helped him to protect the sheep in his charge. This gift and talent came from God for the good of his family's business. There is no doubt that practice and diligence improved these God-given talents. This kind of gift is common—for the common good.

As David perched himself on a high rock and sat in the shade to watch over the sheep, he sang his songs of praise and worship. He came to understand that the sheep in his charge were not just any old sheep, but they belonged to God who put them in his care as a steward.[10] Because he knew the sheep belonged to God Almighty, he knew God would protect the sheep and defend him in his duty. This confidence in Yehovah God as Protector and Provider strengthened him to rise up in the power of the Spirit and rescue his lambs from the mouth of the lions. When the lion turned on him, David killed it by the strength of the Spirit of a holy God who worked through this shepherd boy to protect and provide for his family. God's power and might became apparent in David's weakness.

---
10. Genesis 9:3, Deuteronomy 8:18, Psalm 8:6–9; 24:1, 2 Corinthians 9:8.

In a culture that exalted the eldest son as the first evidence of a father's strength, ruddy little David was considered the least of the brothers. They looked down on the youngest as the weakest branch of the family tree. But this unlikely kid slayed lions by the power of the Spirit who was upon him. It's worth saying again for emphasis: God didn't strengthen David's body to make him a muscle-bound superhero type strong enough to slay a bear. Instead, this truth teaches us that God often chooses to use the least of us for His power and might to shine out. David's battle with a giant of a man is a great picture of this truth.

David prepared himself to step out against Goliath in the same way he attacked the lion and bear that came after his lambs. When King Saul gave David his armor to protect him in battle, he found it too cumbersome. But the armor of God fit perfectly. It's important to get the whole picture. Goliath was a lifelong warrior who was nine-foot tall. The armor and weapons he carried weighed three times what David weighed. But this featherweight shepherd boy went out against Goliath in the power and strength of the Spirit. He knew the LORD already won the victory because this oversized man defied the troops of a holy God; the army of a holy nation. David saw Goliath as a man who stood against God's good purpose and plan.

The scene was set. The least regarded, and least likely boy with no battle experience against an oversized brute—a lifelong warrior. A boy with a slingshot against a hulk of a man with sword, spear, javelin, and shield. Hands down, the crowd placed their bets on Goliath. David's stone didn't kill Goliath, but it knocked him down. Then David finished the job with the giant's own weapons. God manifested His power in David's weakness, and the LORD won the victory and all the glory.

Consider the impossible odds. No doubt David's three brothers stopped breathing as they watched their cheeky little brother go out against that grizzled warrior. But David knew the presence of a holy God and he knew God would give Israel the victory. He went into battle as a skilled and diligent shepherd boy with a talent for shepherding the family's sheep. This was his common gift. Killing predators and giants with five times his strength was his spiritual gift. He stepped out with confidence knowing where he stood before a holy God because he was anointed--gifted for fighting that boastful brute. He knew the work God had given him to do, and he fought this battle in the power of the Spirit. He killed Goliath in the name of the LORD, and this victory was holy unto the LORD.

It's good for Christians to request God's help to make their plans work out. It's an everyday practice for us to pray and ask for God's help in the common work we do to support our families. We do what is right and good when we work at our job as if we worked for the LORD. As the Apostle Paul said,

> *Whatever you do, work at it with all your heart,*
> *as working for the Lord, not for human masters.*
>
> (Colossians 3:23)

Put your heart into the job God provided for you, because this is excellent in every way. But to accomplish the work of the church, the kingdom of heaven, and the Great Commission in this final leg of the race, we need the gifts and power of the Spirit of Jesus to make us instruments through whom God's power is manifested. And the work of the Spirit through God's people is holy before the LORD.

Here we find the need for a great separation between holy and common. A clear distinction of purpose must be made between God-given strength, wisdom, abilities for common use, and the power of a holy God at work through weak vessels to accomplish His good eternal purpose and plan.

Strength of body, wisdom, education, and natural abilities are excellent. God gives them in varying degrees to all mankind for the common good of families, society, and commerce. But they are not the means to accomplish the work of the kingdom of heaven's holy and eternal purpose. For all of Jesus' followers, it is not a matter of "making it happen" with God helping us. Instead, we serve and minister the very heart of God, in the power and might of the Holy Spirit of Righteousness, to accomplish all that He has purposed and planned through His weak sheep. God manifests His power and might through frail vessels who are separated to a holy God. We step up to worship and we serve in the little strength we have and then the Lord Almighty rises up in power to accomplish His good work through us. We serve as His hand extended and the Almighty receives all the glory.

An Example of Separating Holy from Common

> *While they were eating, Jesus took bread, and when he had given thanks, he broke it and gave it to his disciples, saying, "Take it; this is my body." Then he took a cup, and when he had given thanks, he gave it to them, and they all drank from it. "This is my blood of the covenant, which is poured out for many," he said to them. "Truly I tell you, I will not drink again from the fruit of the vine until that day when I drink it new in the kingdom of God." When they had sung a hymn,*
> *they went out to the Mount of Olives.*
>
> (Mark 14:22–26)

There is one means of worship that is most universal and familiar to Christian churches, and that is partaking of Christ in communion. Because we are all familiar with the Table of the LORD, the bread and the cup, this section focuses on the importance of separating what is holy from what is common as we come into Christ Jesus' holy presence to worship before the LORD. We will also discover that separating holy from common is not the same as separating what is holy from what is unholy.

First, let's look at who we are and how we are made. We are created in God's image as three-part beings. The first part is the body that God made out of the dust of the ground. The second part is spirit, brought to life by the wind of the Spirit breathed into the first Adam's created body. The third part is the soul that came into being as body (dust) and spirit (breath) came together. God created Adam, and then breathed into him the breath of life and he became a living soul.[11]

We, like Adam and Eve, consist of body, soul, and spirit. The body is the part of us that functions in this natural world, and is affected by gravity to keep our feet on the ground. The soul is each person's unique personality, and gives each of us our own special way of hearing, seeing, smelling, tasting, and touching. The spirit of a person is the part of us that is able to connect to the spiritual realm—the invisible realm that surrounds us; the kingdom of heaven. Our redeemed spirit makes it possible for us to walk in the Spirit. As Paul admonishes us:

So I say, walk by the Spirit, and you will not gratify the desires of the flesh.

(Galatians 5:16)

Body, soul, and spirit are the three parts of our one being that God has created in His image. How does all this come together when we are called to separate what is holy from what is common as we worship, serve and minister? How is it possible for a three-part being (body, soul, and spirit) to separate what is holy from what is common? At this point it is important to understand how our three parts interact in the realm of the kingdom of heaven. To partake of abundant blessings of Communion in the fullness of the Spirit of Jesus, our spirit needs to be enlightened by the word. We are called to be diligent Bible students to fortify our spirit to take the lead over the soul and body. The Apostle Paul instructs us to discipline the body to subject our body as a slave.[12] In this way, the body becomes subject to our soul and spirit.

It helps us to understand that in a very real sense our common feet are set

---

11. A study of the three-part nature of our being is covered separately in chapter eight.
12. 1 Corinthians 9:27.

upon terra firma, while our spiritual feet stand in the kingdom of heaven. Our natural hand receives common blessings—our daily bread that God provides for all humankind.

> *For he makes his sun rise on the evil and on the good,*
> *and sends rain on the just and on the unjust.*
>
> (Matthew 5:45 ESV)

Conversely, holy hands[13] receive the Bread of Life—an eternal blessing. Our strengthened soul and spirit cause the body to cooperate in worship to receive spiritual gifts—gifts of the kingdom of heaven.

> *Every good and perfect gift is from above, coming down from the Father of the*
> *heavenly lights, who does not change like shifting shadows.*
>
> (James 1:17)

Worship that is spiritual and real is not initiated in the mortal body. Instead, true worship is by means of the Spirit of Jesus poured out into our spirit. Then our spirit inspires us to lift holy hands in worship. In spirit we bow before a holy God. Our knees bend down to pray by the leading of our spirit, in the Spirit. Outward expressions of worship are an outpouring of and a reflection of worship from our heart and spirit.

With our common feet on the ground and spiritual feet set in God's kingdom, we partake of the LORD Jesus in covenant with Christ at the Lord's Supper. It's as if our common hands accept the bread, and holy hands receive the true body of Jesus. It is as if common hands receive a cup, and holy hands receive and partake of the true blood of Christ. In a very real sense, in partaking of Christ, what takes place in the common realm is an outward expression of and a reflection of a greater reality that takes place in our spirit in Jesus' holy presence.

The soul part of us comes together for its part in receiving Communion. A person's soul gives each of us a unique and special sense of the work Christ accomplishes in us as we partake. One of us may have a sense of jubilance—knowing God's forgiveness and mercy in the moment. Another may be grieved over their sin and brought to repentance and forgiveness. Still another may have a sense of peace wash over them, as if led beside still waters—a soul restored. And for another, a sense of assurance—faith and confidence in Christ Jesus' healing touch. These things are matters of the soul under the leading and covering of our spirit that is led by the Holy Spirit.

---

13. 1 Timothy 2:8.

The spirit of a person is the principal partaker of Holy Communion. In spirit we enter Christ's living, active presence to be partakers of the true body and blood of our LORD and Savior, Jesus Christ. In the spirit we eat of Christ's body, and drink of His blood. This is not symbolic, but a spiritual reality that affects us for all eternity. The Patriarch Jacob laid hands on his son, Judah, and prophesied, looking forward to Christ and the church's great celebration

> *He will tether his donkey to a vine, his colt to the choicest branch;*
> *he will wash his garments in wine, his robes in the blood of grapes.*
> (Genesis 49:11)

To receive, share and partake of Communion in this manner is separating what is holy from what is common. Both holy and common have a part, both are necessary, but they are held separate—not to confuse one with the other.

When we limit partaking of the Lord's Table only in body, the bread and cup are merely symbolic. If we partake without distinguishing what is holy from what is common, we are in danger of defaulting to common flesh. In this default mode we may eventually act like the people in Corinth who came to the table in an unholy manner as inconsiderate gluttons and drunks.[14] The Corinthians selfish, self-serving appetites are an obvious example of not separating what is holy from what is unholy.

First we must separate what is holy from fleshly desires that are unholy. Then we are called to separate what is holy from what is common and partake of Holy Communion in spirit and truth. When we separate what is holy from what is common, we enter into spiritual and real worship. It's like opening the floodgates. When we worship before the LORD, separating what is common from what is holy, our worship is in harmony with God's orderly creation. What is common must be subordinate to what is holy. As we worship, serve and minister, our mortal body ought to be subject to soul and spirit. In this way we manifest Jesus' living and active presence in the power of the Spirit of Christ.[15]

Place the Light on a Lampstand

First, we learned that the light of the first day of creation is greater than the light of the fourth day. It's the light of the kingdom of heaven, and an eternal light. The light of the fourth day is for the common good of all humankind and will cease to shine out at the end of time. Jesus spoke of this day to His disciples.

---
14. 1 Corinthians 11:17–34.
15. Ezekiel 42:20; 44:23.

Immediately after the distress of those days "the sun will be darkened, and the moon will not give its light; the stars will fall from the sky, and the heavenly bodies will be shaken."

(Matthew 24:29)

We came to see a clear and distinct difference in the purpose and effect of the first day's light and the fourth day's light. The light of the first day of creation affects us for all eternity, while the light of the fourth day is common light to warm the earth. This separation of light is important because Christians are called to walk in the light of the first day, while all humankind enjoys the light of the fourth day. Our spirit is strengthened and enlightened in the word through the Holy Spirit's work, and this is the work of the first day's light. We must not rely upon what is weak and common to accomplish what is only possible by means of the Spirit. This proves to be true as we see that God's power is best manifested in weak vessels, as illustrated in shepherd boy David's life.[16]

What is common is good in its place for its purpose, but must be separated from what is holy to complete the work of the Great Commission. First we must separate what is holy from what is unholy, and then we are ready to separate what is holy from what is common to enter into worship, service, and ministries that are only possible by the anointing, gifting, and empowering work of the Spirit of Jesus. This makes it possible for us to powerfully serve in weak vessels that manifest the living, active presence of our LORD Jesus in the strength and authority of the Spirit. As we enter into light that is holy, holding it separate from light that is common, we enter into worship that is spiritual and real.

---

16. 2 Corinthians 12:9.

Chapter 4
The Pathway of Light
Q & A

1. Describe a great weakness of the modern-day American church.

2. Why are God's people compared to sheep rather than lions?

3. Why does the Bible teach that God's power is best manifested in weak vessels?

4. What is needed today to finish the work of the Great Commission?

My Journal Notes:

Chapter 5:
The Measuring Rod

Key Scriptures:

- "The angel who talked with me had a measuring rod of gold to measure the city, its gates and its walls." (Revelation 21:15)
- "Examine yourselves, to see whether you are in the faith. Test yourselves. Or do you not realize this about yourselves, that Jesus Christ is in you?—unless indeed you fail to meet the test!" (2 Corinthians 13:5 ESV)

There are various rods in the Old and New Testaments that offer us a greater understanding of God's good work in people's lives from the beginning of time. The Scriptures show several rods for measuring, as well as for many other purposes. For our study we will focus on rods as the rod of a leader and shepherd, measuring rod, measuring reed, plumb line, rod as a standard for judgment, a rod of accounting, a rod of discipline, and last, a rod of mercy that measures for rebuilding.

When the Scriptures on the topic of God's measuring rod are brought together, we find comfort in knowing God's standard of measure. We are reassured by God's righteous and just judgments against the world's darkness that would otherwise destroy His children. This standard of measure gives Christians the means to separate what is holy from what is common, so that we may worship, serve, and minister in the fullness of Christ. God's standard also provides the means to examine ourselves as the Apostle Paul teaches us.

From Genesis to Revelation, measurements are made with scales, cups, plumb lines, cords, and other standards of measure. In Genesis chapter 15, the sin of the Amorites was measured. The prophet Amos measured with a plumb line. Ezekiel wrote about the LORD's messenger with his writing case in hand to take an inventory of Jerusalem's sin.[1] The Father gave the Holy Spirit to Jesus without measure or limit—an immeasurable anointing.[2] Ezekiel's temple was measured in great detail,[3] and in the 21st chapter of Revelation a golden rod measures the Holy City.

It's important to understand why, throughout time, so many things are carefully measured. In this chapter, we will focus on a few measuring rods even though there are many different "rods" mentioned in Scripture. Beginning with the prophetic words written by Isaiah, we'll focus on measuring rods scripture by scripture, like taking steps on a trek through the Bible.

---
1. Ezekiel 9:11.
2. John 3:34.
3. Ezekiel 40.

All the instruments used to test, weigh, and measure offer vital standards when it comes to separating. It was necessary to measure and take account—like taking an inventory. The ancient kings are an example. After they were victorious in battle, they took an account before dividing up the spoils of war so that each soldier could receive what was due him.

Our first step teaches us about a reed to measure out justice.

A "reed," קָנֶה *qaneh*, is used as a measuring stick—a rod of justice. In the ancient times, a master builder would make his own measuring rod that became the standard for everything he built. Like a yardstick or meter stick, he used it as a standard. Isaiah prophesied of Jesus who would come as Master Builder to walk among us and establish His church. As Master Builder, Jesus held to the long-established standard of measure. He, like John the Baptist, didn't break, bruise, or bend the measuring rod for His own purpose. God's holiness, as revealed in Jesus Christ, remains as the standard by which everything is measured. The Apostle Peter revealed God's standard when he wrote God's command:

Be holy, because I am holy.

(1 Peter 1:16)

God gave the Law to Israel, holy words written on stone tablets, as a standard to separate them as a holy nation. The Law of Shabbat is one example of this standard:

Also I gave them my Sabbaths as a sign between us,
so they would know that I the Lord made them holy.

(Ezekiel 20:12)

But it wasn't the adherence to man-made Shabbat traditions that made them holy. The Law was a sign, an impossible standard that separated them to Messiah—their Yeshua HaMashiach in whose rest they were made holy. Our victorious Savior is the standard of measure that can never be broken. Jesus made this clear, saying,

Do not think that I have come to abolish the Law or the Prophets;
I have not come to abolish them but to fulfill them.

(Matthew 5:17)

God's holiness remains the standard of measure, and yet none of us, on our own, measures up to God's holiness, let alone the requirements of the Law. Jesus' work on the cross brought us into His kingdom of grace, mercy, forgiveness of sins, healing, and restoration—so that we might overcome by the blood of the Lamb. He brought us into the Light of Life, and by His abundant grace He delivered us from the curse of the Law. God's standard of measure is Jesus Christ, who reveals to us His immeasurable love and abundant mercies.

This standard of measure, the reed, shows us that we cannot measure up apart from Christ, who is the perfect standard. It is our LORD Jesus who portions out justice, always with forgiveness and mercy. When the measure of sin would overwhelm God's people, judgment is measured out in order to bring people back into creation's perfect order.

And the Lord asked me, "What do you see, Amos?"
"A plumb line," I replied. Then the Lord said, "Look, I am setting a plumb line among my people Israel; I will spare them no longer."

(Amos 7:8)

A "plumb line," אֲנָךְ *anak*, is a tool used to ensure that a vertical wall is true to plumb, i.e. straight up and down. When a wall doesn't measure up, the rickety wall is torn down so that it can be rebuilt straight and true. The prophet Amos speaks of God's people being measured to prepare for corrective discipline. The angel of the LORD showed the prophet Zechariah a measuring basket to weigh the sins of an apostate people.[4] The prophets' messages showed God's good purpose in discipline, to pour out His mercy and bring His people back once again as a holy nation separated to the LORD.

When a plumb line or measuring rod showed that work must be done, but then the work was refused, the rod of correction would come to do its good work. And it was certainly a good work because God's purpose was to show their need of Christ and to drive them back into the Good Shepherd's fold—back to true worship and fellowship. The lessons about the measurements of a plumb line were also taught in Jesus' parable of a fruit tree:

He cuts off every branch in me that bears no fruit,
while every branch that does bear fruit he prunes so that it will be even more fruitful.

(John 15:2)

Every tree that does not bear good fruit is cut down and thrown into the fire.

(Matthew 7:19)

Bushel[5] baskets are often used to measure the harvest from an orchard tree. A tree that produces many bushels of fruit will be pruned to make it

---

4. Zechariah 5:6.
5. A bushel of apples is 42 to 48 lbs.

more fruitful. But if the bushel basket is empty, the tree no longer measures up. Because it produced no fruit, it will be cut down and thrown into the fire.

The plumb line and the bushel basket show us the need to measure ourselves by the standard of God's word to encourage us to be fruitful branches of the true Vine, who is our LORD Jesus. When we don't measure up, we see our need of Christ who measured up on our behalf.

I saw a wall completely surrounding the temple area. The length of the measuring rod in the man's hand was six long cubits, each of which was a cubit and a handbreadth. He measured the wall; it was one measuring rod thick and one rod high.

(Ezekiel 40:5)

A "measuring rod," מִדָּה *middâh*, is revealed in Ezekiel's vision. He was shown a rod in the hands of a man who glowed like burnished brass.[6] Jesus Christ wields the rod because He is the measure of holiness. Ezekiel revealed the temple—a type of the church that Christ Jesus that was established after His death and resurrection. The temple Ezekiel saw was constructed according to the rod Jesus holds in His hands, because He is the standard, the measure of all things. The Psalmist wrote about this standard:

Righteousness and justice are the foundation of your throne;
love and faithfulness go before you.

(Psalm 89:14)

Why is it so important for God's prophet Ezekiel to see the detailed measuring of the temple, and record the measurements for us to see? The temple of worship was revealed to establish God's promise to restore Israel to their native land. The vision of the temple revealed God victorious in the Church to come. The temple walls must be measured to be sure they were constructed to standard, strong and firm for God's children.

And I tell you that you are Peter, and on this rock I will build my church, and the gates of Hades will not overcome it.

(Matthew 16:18)

Yeshua, our Savior, is an unswerving standard of measure to offer the comfort of God's loving arms that shelters all who will gather in His holy presence to worship, serve, and minister.

As John's disciples were leaving, Jesus began to speak to the crowd about John: "What did you go out into the wilderness to see? A reed swayed by the wind?"

(Matthew 11:7)

---
6. Daniel 10:6, Revelation 1:15.

The "reed," κάλαμος *kalamos*, is revealed to us in John the Baptizer who proclaimed the Messiah to come. He was not swayed or shaken by the wind. The bold oracles he proclaimed were the beginning of the Gospel message that would be preached throughout the world. John stood firm in his faith; he was resolute, not changing with the winds of doctrine, not swayed by religious teachings of his day. He held to an unwavering standard, and we can learn from his example.

Then we will no longer be infants, tossed back and forth by the waves, and blown here and there by every wind of teaching and by the cunning and craftiness of people in their deceitful scheming.

(Ephesians 4:14)

The Gospel message is true, and right—it has not changed. The Good News of God's saving grace is a steadfast standard for all that is preached and taught. We come to hear the Gospel like bruised reeds, and we're made strong in saving faith.

A bruised reed he will not break, and a smoldering wick he will not snuff out. In faithfulness he will bring forth justice.

(Isaiah 42:3)

The Law provides a measurement that shows us our sin and depravity, and therefore our need of Christ. When we examine ourselves, the righteousness of Christ Jesus is the standard of measure. For all who will hear, the Good News Gospel message brings us into Christ who fulfilled the law. Now, in Christ, we meet God's standard of holiness. He calls us to dwell in Him, to stand in His council, to abide in His presence, and remain in Him so that we may be a holy people—wholly in Christ. And in Christ, our Heavenly Father will always see us as measuring up. In Christ we are accepted as meeting the standard of perfection.

We come to Christ bruised and broken, and He was broken that our brokenness might be healed. Jesus will not snuff out the last spark of hope that remains in us. Instead, He brings our hearts to repentance, shows us mercy and forgiveness, and receives us as His own. Our Lord Jesus is the Bridegroom who receives us with great joy. John the Baptizer, and John the great Revelator proclaimed Christ without wavering before a people who were hungry to hear the Gospel of His saving grace. Our Lord Jesus has provided the means to meet the standard in the Good News Gospel.

The city was laid out like a square, as long as it was wide. He measured the city with the rod and found it to be 12,000 stadia in length, and as wide and high as it is long.

(Revelation 21:16)

The "measure," μέτρον *metron*, assures us we will enter into the joy of the Lord, knowing that every precious building stone in God's holy city is measured—fully prepared to receive His bride. Until that day the Spirit who indwells us is not limited by our own righteousness, but abundantly poured out as the righteousness of Jesus Christ. The term "without measure" means the work is of eternal value—its effect is beyond the limits of time and space. The work of those God calls is accomplished in the supernatural, invisible realm and is of immeasurable, eternal quality. Indeed, eternity cannot be measured. Truly, God's created universe cannot be measured. This is the measure of the Spirit given to those who are called to utter the words the Almighty speaks, and to be Jesus' hands extended to those in need.

For he whom God has sent utters the words of God, for he gives the Spirit without measure.

(John 3:34 ESV)

The Good Shepherd has His rod in hand to separate what is holy, eternal, and infinite from what is common, temporal, material, and limited. This rod is the great separator that makes it possible for us to discern what is holy from what is common as we are empowered to minister, serve, and worship before a holy God.

I will make you pass under the rod, and I will bring you into the bond of the covenant.

(Ezekiel 20:37 ESV)

This is the righteous standard by which everything is weighed. The religious leaders of Jesus' day were weighed and came up short. They kept to the letter of the Law and forgot the spirit of God's standards. The Word of righteousness is the standard, and when Jesus saw the inside of the Pharisees' cups, they were cauldrons of corruption and evil. They were like their fathers who were measured and found to overflow with violence and bloodshed. Jesus still holds this two-edged sword[7] in His hand and uses it to separate His people to Himself, no longer corrupted by the filth of hypocrisy and evil, and the sins of the fathers.

At the end of time, each of us will be held up to the standard of righteousness, our Lord Jesus Christ. Those who reject Christ will be separated like "goats" into eternal darkness. For those who are in Christ, the rod of the Good Shepherd will be used to separate to Himself all the sheep of His pasture.

---
7. Matthew 10:34, Hebrews 4:12.

No longer will there be any cause to weep, nor any cause for sorrow.

> *Therefore this is what the Lord says: "I will return to Jerusalem with mercy, and there my house will be rebuilt. And the measuring line will be stretched out over Jerusalem,"*
> *declares the Lord Almighty.*
> (Zechariah 1:16)

The "scepter," שֵׁבֶט shebet, was placed in King Solomon's hand and shows us the purpose of this rod—to lead God's people with wisdom. This wisdom became very real when two mothers came before Solomon with one dead baby and one living child. They both claimed the living child. The king applied the rod of wisdom to separate the truth from a lie to reunite the child with his real mother.[8] Solomon applied a scepter of wisdom and justice as Yehovah's anointed to serve and lead His people.

> *Your throne, O God, will last forever and ever,*
> *a scepter of justice will be the scepter of your kingdom.*
> (Psalm 45:6)

King Solomon served the cause of justice with words of wisdom, threatening a sword and then applying a ruler's scepter to discern what was right. He wielded it to return the child to his rightful mother, and to send the unlawful mother away so she could do no more harm.

This is a rod that serves to measure, to judge and separate the sheep from the goats. The rod serves to comfort those who are called to be the sheep of God's pasture.[9] And the rod also serves as a rod of judgment against the "goats."[10] This is a beautiful display of God's abundant grace and mercy. The Good Shepherd, like King Solomon, uses His rod to judge and to separate those He has called out of darkness into the light—the bond of His everlasting covenant. This is the fulfillment of His immeasurable love for those who are called by His holy name. But for those who scoff at the Good Shepherd's call, judgment is measured out.

> *Thus you witness against yourselves that you are sons of those who murdered the prophets. Fill up, then, the measure of your fathers.*
> (Matthew 23:31–32 ESV)

---

8. 1 Kings 3:16–28.
9. Psalm 100:3.
10. Psalm 2:9.

Jesus proclaimed seven woes upon the entrenched religious leaders in Israel. The Pharisees and teachers of the Law were corrupt rulers who protected their personal interests. They established a self-serving religious monopoly that stood against what God had intended for His holy nation. They took great care to clean and polish the outside of their "cups" for everyone to see and admire, while on the inside filth and violence brewed.[11] Our LORD Jesus is a just and righteous judge, an unwavering reed who sees through the exterior polish to the inside of the cup.

He rules the world in righteousness and judges the peoples with equity.

(Psalm 9:8)

The "measure," קָו Qav, is the standard for mercy. The LORD God Almighty reached out with an abundance of mercy as He prepared to measure the city of Jerusalem and prepare for rebuilding. He had measured the people's sin and brought them to judgment—but with the good purpose of restoring them as a holy nation before God. Again and again God measured the walls to be sure His people were protected. But when God's people stepped outside the shelter of the Most High, the LORD measured them, and found them wanting. Then He brought the rod of correction upon them, and finally in His abundant mercy brought them to repentance to be restored again within His walls of protection. Jerusalem was measured to be sure it would provide a place for all God's restored people, so that once again they could be a holy nation before Him. This was a preview of what God is preparing for us. We have the promise of an eternal home; a holy city that is measured to be sure it's fully prepared as the bride of Christ.

And yet because of our many failings, we come with contrite hearts, confessing our sin, our weaknesses, and our need of Christ. In the same way that God restored the Israelites to Jerusalem, He pours out His abundant mercies upon repentant hearts today to restore us to the fullness of Christ in all our worship, service, and ministries before a holy God. We have this great hope, because over and over throughout all of Scripture we see God's mercy prevailing over judgment. One great example of this loving kindness is the prophetic proclamation of the prophet Zechariah, who announced the restoration of Yehovah's people. The following verses show a clear pattern of grace and mercy:

This is what the Lord Almighty says: "Now hear these words,
Let your hands be strong so that the temple may be built."

(Zechariah 8:9)

---

11. Matthew 23:26.

God's judgments inflicted hard times on the people, but God was merciful and faithful to restore, and deliver them from the trap of sin. God's people were captives in their sin, but He released them to rebuild the temple of worship to His holy name.

Before that time there were no wages for people or hire for animals.

(Zechariah 8:10)

God brought their hearts to repentance, forgave them, cleansed them and once again brought His people into the land that flowed with milk and honey.[12] In forgiveness and mercy, the Great I AM restored them to favor.

"But now I will not deal with the remnant of this people as I did in the past," declares the Lord Almighty.

(Zechariah 8:11)

God restored them to the land of promise, their property, their villages, and once again poured out His abundant blessings on His people.

The seed will grow well, the vine will yield its fruit, the ground will produce its crops, and the heavens will drop their dew.

(Zechariah 8:12)

Jerusalem and the temple of worship became the central focus of their return home. This was key to the whole plan of restoration—to worship God in His holy temple in Jerusalem according to all holiness. God strengthened them for the task of rebuilding that was ahead of them.

Do not be afraid, but let your hands be strong.

(Zechariah 8:13)

Jesus calls out to us with words of forgiveness, mercy, and restoration. In all that God is doing among His people today, His words of mercy are for the good purpose of restoring our temples[13] in His family of fellowship. Once again, we will gather together to worship, serve and minister before the LORD in all holiness. God's good purpose remains the same as He rescues and restores us to true temple worship.

To rescue us from the hand of our enemies, and to enable us to serve him without fear in holiness and righteousness before him all our days.

(Luke 1:74–75)

---

12. Numbers 13:27.
13. (1 Corinthians 13:16).

The final "measurement" is μετρέω *metréō*.[14] This measuring made sure the city, whose builder and Maker is God, is fully prepared as God's holy dwelling place. This final dwelling must measure up to what God planned from the beginning for all His adopted sons and daughters. This is the fulfillment of all God desires for His people—the place where we will dwell together with Him for all eternity.

In ancient Jewish tradition, a betrothed son would prepare a place for the wife he was pledged to marry. This wedding tradition foreshadowed Jesus' promise to return.

And if I go and prepare a place for you,
I will come back and take you to be with me that you also may be where I am.

(John 14:3)

But even the son didn't know the time and date he would be wedded. The son would not bring his bride home until the father assessed the son's preparations and declared it to be ready.

But about that day or hour no one knows, not even the angels in heaven,
nor the Son, but only the Father.

(Matthew 24:36)

The Father called for the work of the bridegroom to be evaluated to assure it was ready to receive the bride, prepared for the wedding feast. In the same way, the holy city will be measured with a golden rod[15] to be sure it is prepared as a His bride, and to prove the city is consecrated in every part according to the Father's holy standard. The walls of the city will be measured to show that it is ready, the bride of Christ fully adorned for the Bridegroom. We will be forever protected and separated from all weeping and grief. We will be shielded from all things that would be cause for sorrowful tears.

So that they may have the full measure of my joy within them.

(John 17:13)

The Heart of the Matter

In the twenty-fifth year of Israel's exile,[16] on the tenth day of the first month, the hand of the LORD took Ezekiel to the land of Israel in a vision. God set his feet set on a very high mountain. He saw a man "whose appear-

---

14. μετρέω *metréō*, to measure out.
15. Revelation 21:15.
16. Approximately 574 BC.

ance was like bronze" standing in the gateway with a linen cord and a measuring rod in his hand. The next four chapters of Ezekiel describe in great detail the precise measurements of the new temple, with each measurement carefully noted.

The measurements were precisely recorded for a good purpose. The Old Covenant priests and Levites were called to separate themselves from what was common[17] in order to be faithful as they worshipped and served in the holy temple, following God's requirements to the letter. Their lawful requirements illustrate for us how we are to follow the Spirit of Christ to bring order to our worship. For them and for us the temple of worship is measured for one purpose: to separate holy from common in the temple. The temple Ezekiel saw was measured to keep separate—what is holy in its rightful place and what is common in its proper place.

Both holy and common are useful, but must be held separate—each for its own good purpose. It's like the oil we put in the crankcase for lubrication, and fuel we put in the tank to power the engine. Each serves its purpose, but don't get them mixed up. We, like the priests who served in the Old Testament temple, must separate what is holy and what is common as we serve before the LORD in today's temple, which is a gathering of the body of Christ. Ezekiel chapter 44 gives a clear instruction that those who enter to worship must be circumcised in "heart and flesh." The Law of circumcision is another means for the Spirit to teach us that spirit and flesh must be separated as we worship, serve, and minister before the LORD. This separation fulfills the spirit of the law.

When the temple measurements were completed, God instructed Ezekiel to have God's people "consider the plan." The original Hebrew reveals that the LORD was saying: "Let them measure and evaluate to see the perfection of the plan."[18] The purpose was to bring the people to stand in awe before a righteous God, and be ashamed of their sin as they considered the design, arrangement, exits, entrances, and the LORD's plan for worship.[19] Jehovah God instructed Ezekiel to "make known" God's design to the people only when their hearts came to repentance. Then they could, once again, enter into the joy of their salvation.

This is a vital truth. The Ezekiel temple measurements illustrate the importance for us to separate what is holy from what is common. For those who make this separation, their service will be most effective and powerful in the Spirit of Christ. In Ezekiel's day, after the temple was measured to be sure

---
17. Ezekiel 44:23.
18. Ezekiel 43:10.
19. Ezekiel 43:11.

that holy and common were separate, God's glory returned to the temple like a tsunami wave, with a voice like the roar of rushing waters, in glorious and radiant light.

> *Then the Spirit lifted me up and brought me into the inner court, and the glory of the Lord filled the temple.*
>
> (Ezekiel 43:5)

God has not changed. His glory and this truth still apply today. Ezekiel's words appeal to us in the present. We must apply the holy Scriptures as a measuring rod to separate what is holy from what is common. This is a rod, staff, scepter, and plumb line for all who are included in the priesthood of believers. All who will minister and serve according to all holiness are called to separate what is holy from what is common. The eternal work of the church, the kingdom of heaven, and the Great Commission can be accomplished no other way.

This is a call to take up the scepter of leadership, to shepherd God's people in holiness— counting our common gifts as nothing. We must not rely on our ordinary talents and accomplishments because they simply don't measure up for the Great Commission task ahead of us. In our Christian faith, we are called to take an account of ourselves to see if we meet God's standard of holiness.[20] In leadership, we are called to take an account of our flock using God's word as the standard of measure.[21] To minister and serve before a holy God we must not do so by our "sweat"[22] but by means of the anointing, gifting, and empowering work of the Spirit of Jesus. Like the Master Builder, we need a rod to use as a standard measure so that we can separate what is holy from what is common. Christ Jesus, the Word, has met the standard for He is perfect in all holiness. In Christ we will worship, serve, and minister in the everlasting richness of kingdom light.[23]

We have all failed to separate what is holy from what is common as we worship and serve. In the church today, too often we depend on our own resources, our own strength and abilities to accomplish the work of the Great Commission. This self-reliance is like a mountain-sized obstacle to keep us from accomplishing the work given to us. But this mighty mountain will become level ground, because a kingdom-sized bulldozer is making a highway for the remnant of God's people.

---

20. 2 Corinthians 13:5.
21. Proverbs 27:23–24.
22. Ezekiel 44:18.
23. Colossians 1:12.

> *"Not by might nor by power, but by my Spirit," says the Lord Almighty.*
> (Zechariah 4:6)

Christ Jesus is our great hope. With an outpouring of abundant mercy and forgiveness, He restores us to accomplish this good work. And His glory will once again fill our temples of worship.

> *And the glory of the Lord filled the temple.*
> (Ezekiel 43:5)

Chapter 5
The Measuring Rod
Q & A

1. What is the standard of measure for a godly life?

2. What purpose was served in measuring the holy city in the book of Revelation?

3. Why was Ezekiel instructed to have the people consider the plan of the temple after it was measured?

4. What occurred after holy and common were separated in Ezekiel's temple?

My Journal Notes:

Chapter 6:
I Can Do It

Key Scriptures:

- "Now listen, you who say, 'Today or tomorrow we will go to this or that city, spend a year there, carry on business and make money.' Why, you do not even know what will happen tomorrow. What is your life? You are a mist that appears for a little while and then vanishes." (James 4:13–14)

- "By the grace God has given me, I laid a foundation as a wise builder, and someone else is building on it. But each one should build with care." (1 Corinthians 3:10)

We've all heard people say: "God helps those who help themselves." This motto may be okay when we refer to what is common, but it misses the mark with regard to what is holy. In the work of the Great Commission, there is no human capacity more widespread and useless than self-help. Human types often try to do God's work *for* Him rather than the work God has given us. We tend to be self-confident, self-assured, and full of ourselves when we set out to help God accomplish all that He has purposed and planned. In our arrogance, we think we can add our good ideas to what God has planned, but this is the height of all pride.

We live in a culture that says, "You can be all that you want to be." "Take the bull by the horns and make it happen." These maxims are a part of our values, and when applied in the right way at the right time and for the right purpose—they are helpful.

These motivational quotes serve a purpose, but they are for the common good and must be separated from what is holy. Encouraging words used for the common good must not be confused with what is holy because they have no part in kingdom work, nor do they have a place in the work of ministry that changes lives for all eternity. The work of the Kingdom of Heaven is not a "live *your* dream" kind of work.

To be sure, our personal dreams and goals are good, and God often blesses these dreams for the common good. But when we are brought into God's dream, God's purpose and plan becomes the impetus of our calling, and it will be a work that is holy unto the LORD. God's desire is for His children to be the light of the world just as Jesus taught us.

You are the light of the world.

(Matthew 5:14)

Being light is only possible when the strength of the Spirit is empowered in us. In the Spirit, we are empowered to serve as Jesus' hand extended to those in need of His touch. Creation's beginning in Genesis revealed this separation of holy and common. My Bible study group has heard me repeat, "When you understand the book of Genesis, you will come to a greater understanding of the whole Bible." In fact, it will change your worldview and your view of God's kingdom. In the first book of the Bible, God establishes by His work of creation that He is holy. Now in Christ we are called to holiness.

"Be holy, because I am holy."

(1 Peter 1:16)

As we serve before a holy God, we are called to put aside our common concerns about food, clothes, and shelter, and then minister in the power and strength of the Spirit of Jesus.

Therefore I tell you, do not worry about your life, what you will eat or drink; or about your body, what you will wear. Is not life more than food, and the body more than clothes?

(Matthew 6:25)

The best application of this Scripture is in service and ministry before the LORD. Christian servants are called to cast upon the LORD their common, everyday concerns as they do the work of the kingdom.

To further our study, let's look at a few Biblical characters so we can benefit from their mistakes. From Abel and Abraham to Zerubbabel and Zechariah, our fellow sojourners in the Bible teach us how they messed things up when they tried to accomplish God's work by their own plans and schemes. We'll learn there is no need for us to jump in and attempt to do what only God can do to fulfill His purpose and plan for our lives.

Abram and Sarai, who Yehovah later renamed Abraham and Sarah, took to their own devices to help God fulfill His promise of a son.[1] Sarai had no children and felt the shame her culture inflicted upon childless women. But she had a plan. Sarai gave her maidservant, Hagar, to Abram to have a child in her stead. But this was her own idea, not what God had planned or promised. Abram went along with the scheme. He shared our human weaknesses and must have thought, "I guess I misunderstood God's promise. Let's give this a try so we can have the son God promised."

Their plan brought chaos into Abram's family. Hagar despised Sarai when she realized she was pregnant, and then Sarai blamed Abram for her

---
1. Genesis 16.

troubles. With Abram's permission, Sarai mistreated her maidservant until Hagar fled from the abuse. An angel of the LORD intervened to bring Hagar back, promised her a son to be named Ishmael, who would be a wild donkey of a man and be hostile toward his brothers. Even though Abram and Sarai were not faithful in waiting for God's promise, God remained faithful to fulfill His word to Abraham and Sarah. The LORD gave them Isaac, their son of promise.

As Hagar's son grew, he started to torment Isaac, the son of promise, and Ishmael had to be sent away. Abram and Sarai built upon God's rock-solid promise with straw—that is, their own effort. The long-term consequence of their plan affects us even today. The descendants of Ishmael still live in hostility toward the sons of Isaac.

Rebecca and Jacob took matters into their own hands to fulfill God's promise that the elder son, Esau, would serve the younger son, Jacob. Jacob caught his twin brother in a vulnerable moment when he returned home famished after an all-day hunt. Jacob enticed Esau to sell him the elder son's birthright for a bowl of stew. Esau scorned his birthright—too hungry to care—and accepted the deal. Many years later, when Jacob and Esau's father, Isaac, had taken to his sick bed, old, blind, and ready to pass on, Rebecca and Jacob deceived Isaac in their effort to help God fulfill His promise. Rebecca made the stew Isaac asked his eldest son, Esau, to make. Jacob put goatskins on his arms to make them hairy like his brother. He put on his brother's clothes so he would smell like his brother, and then offered his father his favorite red stew as requested. Jacob deceived his father, Isaac, to steal both the blessing and inheritance of the elder son; a double portion, according to custom. As a result, Jacob ended up fleeing for his life after stealing Esau's blessing and birthright.

> *So he [Jacob] went to him and kissed him. When Isaac caught the smell of his clothes, he blessed him and said, "Ah, the smell of my son is like the smell of a field that the Lord has blessed. May God give you heaven's dew and earth's richness–an abundance of grain and new wine. May nations serve you and peoples bow down to you. Be lord over your brothers, and may the sons of your mother bow down to you. May those who curse you be cursed, and those who bless you be blessed.*
>
> (Genesis 27:27–29)

Moses tried, on his own, to begin the work of freeing Israel from slavery by killing an Egyptian slave master, and then burying him in the sand.[2] He knew God's purpose for his life and took the job in his own hands. Pharaoh

---

2. Exodus 2:1–2.

ordered Moses be killed, and he fled to the wilderness where he spent forty years working as a shepherd. The years in the desert herding sheep were difficult years as a "foreigner in a foreign land."[3] But God used Moses' time as a fugitive for good. During the time in a strange land, God prepared him to lead the nation of Israel out of bondage in Egypt. It took forty years to retrain Moses to become a wise leader, judge, and prophet who performed mighty acts of God to raise up a holy nation before the Lord, and to lead God's people through the wilderness to the Land of Promise.

These heroes of the faith blew it, and all of us can learn from their mistakes. Their stories teach that trying to do God's work for Him in our common strength and ability never works out. There are consequences for attempting to do it our way. But if you have messed up in the past, take heart. There is forgiveness and cleansing in Christ, and quite often God uses our missteps, turning them around for a good purpose. We can take great comfort as we learn from these heroes of the faith, as if they were cheering us on from the grandstands.

Consider this fictitious story of a master builder who was building a house for his family: He gathered a crew to do the work from the ground up to finish. He hired a man named Piloph who was young and energetic, but with very little experience. He only qualified as cleanup man and errand boy. Piloph wanted to impress the boss, so he showed up an hour early on the first day of work to start digging the foundation with his own shovel. An hour later, the rest of the crew showed up with a transit, laser measuring tapes, stakes, line, blueprints, and a backhoe.

"What are you doing?" The master builder looked wide-eyed at Piloph's piles of dirt.

His new clean-up man stood tall and wiped the sweat from his forehead: "I'm digging for the footings."

"But that's not where they go, and that's not how it's done," the master builder said. "But maybe we can use what you dug for a drain line or something."

The message is crystal clear. When we try to do on our own what only the Master Builder can do, without fully understanding the plan, having the wrong tools for the job, and not knowing where the house needs to be built—we mess things up. God doesn't want us to try doing what only He alone can accomplish. He wants us, instead, to do what we are assigned to do,[4] by faith and in obedience, to accomplish our part in God's plan.

---

3. Exodus 2:22.
4. Ephesians 2:10.

We've all blown it by trying to do what only God can do. But even when God's servants are not faithful, even when His servants drop the ball and stumble, God is faithful to forgive us, cleanse us, and set our feet on the solid Rock, Christ Jesus. With our feet on the Rock, we are empowered to accomplish all He desires in and through us in the power of the Spirit. The LORD turns around what we have messed up and makes use of it, and then redirects us to work in accord with His blueprint.

There are three examples in the Bible of people who rose above their common strengths to accomplish the work God ordained for them. Noah, Daniel, and Job are the only people mentioned in the Bible with righteousness sufficient to save, but only themselves.[5] Noah became a lone preacher of righteousness in a depraved world.[6] Daniel, as a captive in a foreign land, would not violate God's law and refused to eat the king's rich foods.[7] Job endured in his faith even while tested with searing painful boils, loss of his children, a wife that told him to "curse God and die," and the finger-pointing from his friends.[8] God worked through each of these heroes of the faith to accomplish His mighty work. Each of them served to fulfill their part in God's master plan. Noah built an ark to save his family and the animals two by two.[9] Daniel served God with honor in a foreign land, and got promoted to serve in a position of great authority.[10] Job endured through great suffering, continued strong in his faith, and was restored to health and prosperity. As he suffered all these trials, he stood up and made one of the greatest declarations of faith:

And after my skin has been destroyed, yet in my flesh I will see God.

(Job 19:26)

The point is that God is more than able to accomplish His purpose and plan. The LORD will choose people to fulfill their part in His plan. The work of God's kingdom will go so much better when we do what we are called and empowered to do by faith, and not try to do what only God can do.

The best of us are guilty of this. We get mixed-up about our job in God's plan. Most of us can say, "Been there, done that." We all get impatient for God to do what we know He has planned to do, and we are quick to jump in and attempt to do what only God can do. We storm the gates of heaven with prayers about the work we know God desires to accomplish. But then we get

---

5. Ezekiel 14:14. (It's a noteworthy dichotomy that even though their righteous acts were sufficient, they could not, and did not, depend on their own righteousness for salvation.)
6. Genesis 6:9.
7. Daniel 1:8.
8. Job 2:9.
9. Genesis 6; 7.
10. Daniel 2:48.

impatient. We get weary in waiting, and we convince ourselves that this must be the right time, and the right way for God's work to get done—and we jump in and attempt to accomplish what only God can do.

Whether in arrogance or ignorance, our plan messes things up. But there's a better way. God will strengthen us as we wait for His plan to unfold.

But they who wait for the Lord shall renew their strength; they shall mount up with wings like eagles; they shall run and not be weary; they shall walk and not faint.

(Isaiah 40:31 ESV)

This is not an inactive, wait-in-line-at-the-coffee-stand kind of waiting. This is an active, strengthening, empowered kind of waiting. The Hebrew word for "wait," קָוָה *qavah,* has connotations of being bound together, like braided strands of a rope.

Now, as you wait, pray, and search the Scriptures your patience grows and you are strengthened. It's as if petitions, waiting on the Lord, and God's word are the fibers used to braid an unbreakable cord. While you're actively waiting, you are bound together with your heavenly Father by the word of God. You are strengthened to draw closer to the heart of God using threads of truth from the Holy Scriptures. As you are strengthened in the Word, the futility of trying to serve in your own strength to accomplish what God alone can do will become more and more obvious. God will use you in your weakness and empower you in the Spirit to accomplish His purpose and plan. Now empowered as His instrument, you will do what is impossible for you and God will receive all the glory and honor for what is accomplished.

Have you noticed that when Jesus performed His miracles, the people gave glory to God? When the blind man's eyes were healed to see, when the deaf man's ears were made to hear, when the paralyzed man was healed, the people gave glory to Yehovah God. They didn't look at Jesus and say, "Wow, this man is so awesome." They looked up and gave glory to God on high. They did so because they were aware that there was no man on earth who could restore eyes to the blind, ears of the deaf, or make lame legs walk again. Jesus was fully man and this is what the people saw as He stretched out his hands to heal. His miracles proved that Jesus was fully God, and fully man.

Only God of creation could do such a mighty work.

When the crowd saw this, they were filled with awe; and they praised God, who had given such authority to man.

(Matthew 9:8)

This is the essence of the matter. When we wait upon the LORD, He renews our strength. That is, the strength of the Spirit is empowered in us, and we will serve as Jesus' hand extended to those in need of His touch. Wandering souls will be restored as we speak Jesus' words of healing.

All this is accomplished in weak vessels by means of the power, gifting, and anointing of the Spirit of Jesus. What God accomplishes will be amazing, just as it was when the Apostle Peter spoke Jesus' name to heal the crippled beggar.

Fellow Israelites, why does this surprise you?
Why do you stare at us as if by our own power or godliness we had made this man walk?

(Acts 3:12)

In Christ, weak vessels step up in the strength of the Almighty. In the power of the Spirit, our worship, service, and ministries are holy before the LORD, and God receives all the glory and honor. Indeed, the LORD's grandeur is best revealed through His servants when we wait on Him and then step out knowing that the Great I AM will use us, weak as we, to reveal His glory, might and power.

Chapter 6
I Can Do It
Q & A

1. What happens when we rely on our own devices, attempting to do what only God can do?

2. When we "blow it," does that also blow God's plan for us?

3. When the people saw Jesus' miracles, they gave glory to God. What inspired them to do so?

My Journal Notes:

Chapter 7: Fire of Separation

Key Scriptures:

- "Be careful not to forget the covenant of the LORD your God that he made with you; do not make for yourselves an idol in the form of anything the LORD your God has forbidden. For the LORD your God is a consuming fire, a jealous God." (Deuteronomy 4:23–24)

- "I will refine them like silver and test them like gold. They will call on my name and I will answer them; I will say, 'They are my people,' and they will say, 'The LORD is our God.'" (Zechariah 13:9)

The Creator of the universe is a consuming fire, and manifests His holy presence in a blaze of glory. Fire in the hands of the Great I AM is awesome in every way. We have touched on the topic of fire already, but in this chapter we will come to see that fire is like the very hand and fingers of God at work in the world.

Most of us have seen or even experienced the terrible destruction of a wildfire and the charred, smoldering remains it leaves behind. Many have also enjoyed the warmth and comfort of a fireplace that drives the winter chill out of our bones. In the same way, heaven's fire is either frightful or comforting. We'll see contrast in the purpose and effects of fire and learn about useless fire. This study explores the Biblical historicity of fire, God's purpose in the use of fire, the effects of fire, and the final revelation of all things through fire. As we look at God's fire, even the fires of judgment, we will see that God's abundant mercies are lavished upon His children.

Fire in Bible History

From the beginning of time, God's holy fire has revealed His awesome power and served His good purpose. In the book of Genesis, an angel brandished a flaming sword at the entrance to the Garden of Eden to guard the way to the Tree of Life. Adam and Eve once enjoyed access to all the trees of the garden except for the tree of knowledge of good and evil—but they wouldn't accept "except." After they overstepped this boundary, God responded with a display of abundant mercy. Even though death held sway in their bodies because of their sin, God covered their nakedness with garments of skin, and then sent them out of their garden paradise. Like a watchman or gatekeeper, an angel brandished a flaming sword to guard the way to the Tree of Life in the garden. And yet God made a way for them through His Son

Jesus, who would be sent to reveal the pathway for all who come to the saving faith. The flaming sword guarded the way, and God made a way through Jesus Christ, His only Son, who is the Tree of Life.

I am the way and the truth and the life. No one comes to the Father except through me.

(John 14:6)

Fire in the hands of a holy God accomplishes his mighty work, to fulfill His word. Throughout history, the LORD Almighty's fire has served to devour the wicked, prove the godly, protect His people, and confirm covenants. In every way, these were the fires of separation to keep God's people from the temptations of a fallen temporal world.

He makes winds his messengers, flames of fire his servants.

(Psalm 104:4)

The fires of heaven have manifested in many ways throughout history. But the best is yet to come. Yehovah God is a wall of fire around Jerusalem to protect His people, the "apple of His eye."[1] The Old Testament prophets looked forward to see God's final triumph. A trek through Bible history will show that fire in the hands of a holy God serves to bring about mighty victories.

To make a binding covenant, God instructed Abraham to cut in half a heifer, a goat, a ram, and also to provide a dove and a pigeon, and then arrange the halves opposite of each other, except for the birds. Then the Lord Almighty instructed Abram.

When the sun had set and darkness had fallen, a smoking firepot with a blazing torch appeared and passed between the pieces. On that day the Lord made a covenant with Abram and said, "To your descendants I give this land."

(Genesis 15:17–18)

Many years later God instructed Abraham, to take his only son Isaac, whom he dearly loved, along with wood and fire to sacrifice his son on God's holy mountain: Mount Moriah. Abraham took Isaac, the heir of promise, to sacrifice him in obedience to Yehovah God. Isaac was his mother's laughter, the hope of the church, the long-awaited son of father Abraham. Abraham knew this and yet acted in obedience. As God renewed His covenant with Abraham, He required a sacrifice. But the LORD, in His abundant mercy, stopped Abraham as he held the knife in hand above Isaac. In an awesome picture of His plan of salvation, God provided a ram caught in the thicket as a substitute. The sacrificial ram foreshadowed Christ as the Passover Lamb

---

1. Zechariah 2:5–9.

and Calvary's sacrificial lamb—God's only Son would be offered up to die in our place, for our sin. Abram offered the provided ram instead; burned upon the wood Isaac carried on his back—a picture of the cross Jesus bore on His back. The offering of Abram's only son foretold of Christ, who, in the fires of affliction, shed His blood, gave His body to be broken, and gave His life, dying in our place to redeem us.[2]

As time went on, the LORD rescued Abraham's nephew, Lot, and his family while ending the scourge of Sodom and Gomorrah's sin with a deluge of fiery sulfur. Out of the fire and burning sulfur, God delivered Lot and his two daughters from the depravity of the people whose abhorrent sins had grieved him.[3]

The Great I AM, the God of Abraham, Isaac, and Jacob appeared to Moses on Mount Horeb in the fire of a bush to call him to lead His chosen people out of slavery. God appeared to him on the mountain's holy ground, ablaze with God's presence.[4]

When God brought Israel out of their slavery in Egypt, He concealed His people with a wall of fire to protect them from the armies of Pharaoh.[5] God's pillar of fire covered the people as they wandered in the wilderness.

By day the Lord went ahead of them in a pillar of cloud to guide them on their way and by night in a pillar of fire to give them light, so they could travel by day or night.

(Exodus 13:21)

After forty years of trials and hardships in the wilderness, God brought the tribes of Israel into the Promised Land through the waters of the Jordan River and the fires of Jericho, the city they plundered and burned.[6]

We went through fire and water, but you brought us to a place of abundance.

(Psalm 66:12)

God sent a fiery chariot to sweep Elijah up to heaven in a whirlwind.

*As they were walking along and talking together,
suddenly a chariot of fire and horses of fire appeared and separated the two of them,
and Elijah went up to heaven in a whirlwind.*

(2 Kings 2:11)

---

2. Genesis 22.
3. Genesis 19:24–28.
4. Exodus 3:2.
5. Exodus 14:24.
6. Joshua 6:24.

The Almighty used Gideon and a few chosen men to defeat the entire Midianite army. Gideon and his troops won the battle by simply lining up around the enemy camp, blowing their trumpets, and then breaking their pottery jars with flaming torches inside.[7] The Lord sent Gideon, saying, "Go in the strength you have" and Yehovah God rose up with mighty strength to save Israel from their oppressors.

The book of Judges is a tragedy—a story of the spiritual wanderings of God's people. But their enemies were defeated when God's people repented of their idolatry and cried out to the Almighty who is faithful. The LORD strengthened Samson to rout the Philistines who oppressed the nation of Israel. In one great victory, Samson caught three hundred foxes, tied their tails in pairs, fastened torches to their tails, and then used them to set the enemies' grain fields on fire.[8] Once again, God's people vanquished their enemies and were delivered by fire.

Shadrach, Meshach, and Abednego were tested and proven like pure refined gold when they were thrown into the king's furnace. The king went into a rage and ordered the fire stoked seven times hotter because they didn't bow down to the statue he created in his honor. But in the roar of flames, the cords that bound them fell away and God delivered them from the furnace without even the scent of smoke on them.[9]

As Jesus taught his disciples, He brought this fire to light. Our Messiah came with a Passion for the cross, and the fire of suffering so that we may come to the cross in saving faith. Now Jesus baptizes His disciples in the fire of the Holy Spirit to gift and empower God's people for servant ministries for the sake of the Gospel.

I have come to bring fire on the earth, and how I wish it were already kindled!

(Luke 12:49)

The fire Jesus proclaimed is the Gospel that divides and separates—father against son, and daughter against mother.[10] The fire of the Gospel separates those who see, hear, believe, and repent from those whose hearts turn away in rebellion as they hear the Gospel message. The Good News came by means of the fires of affliction—the suffering Savior who heard the crowd shout out, "Crucify him, crucify!" The people despised and rejected Him, and through many trials in fires of affliction He became the Chief Cornerstone.

---

7. Judges 7.
8. Judges 15.
9. Daniel 3.
10. Luke 12:53.

The stone the builders rejected has become the cornerstone.

(Psalm 118:22)

Fifty days after Jesus' resurrection from the grave, and ten days after He ascended to the right hand of the Father, the disciples were gathered together to wait for the gift the Father promised through Jesus Christ. They received Jesus' promised gift: a baptism in the fire of the Spirit on the day of Pentecost.[11] Just as promised, the Spirit of Christ came upon them in a baptism of fire.

They saw what seemed to be tongues of fire that separated and came to rest on each of them.

(Acts 2:3)

This awesome gift was poured out upon both men and women. It came like tongues of fire upon those gathered in the room. The fire of the Spirit empowered this little gathering of people to become the Church on that day. They were empowered to carry the Gospel message to the furthest parts of the world.

From the beginning and throughout time, flames and tongues of fire have served to accomplish God's good purpose. From Eden's gate guarded with a flaming sword, the Abrahamic covenant established by fire, a church founded and empowered in the Spirit's fire, and finally the New Jerusalem surrounded by the Almighty as a "wall of fire,"[12] God works by means of fire to establish and confirm covenants, to cover, to protect, to separate, to deliver His called people, and to devour His enemies.

Useless Fire

When God's people minimize or reject the good gifts given in the Spirit, the Church becomes spiritually impoverished. In this deprived state, they are left with little more than common devices to accomplish the work of the Great Commission. The prophet Malachi likened this weakness to "useless fire."

The judges and prophets of Israel were often armed with fire to defeat their enemies. The Church began with a rush of heaven's wind and tongues of fire that came to rest on each of those gathered. And now, in our day, our gatherings for ministry and worship are empowered in the fire of the Spirit of Jesus to complete the work of the Great Commission. We must be aware of the limitations should we attempt to fulfill God's call with useless fire. The Old Testament prophet Malachi spoke out with this stinging indictment

---
11. Acts 1:5.
12. Zechariah 2:5.

against God's people for their futile attempt to do the work of the temple with useless fire:

> *"Oh, that one of you would shut the temple doors, so that you would not light useless fires on my altar! I am not pleased with you," says the Lord Almighty, "and I will accept no offering from your hands."*
>
> (Malachi 1:10)

The prophet's messages were recorded in the Old Testament to instruct us today, and we are dogged with the same weaknesses as the priests and people in Malachi's day. We, like them, are fallible. Too often we try to do the work of the kingdom of heaven in our common strength, talents, and resources. To push forward in the good work on our own is to attempt the work by means of useless fire, and, according to Malachi, we might as well shut the doors and go home.

Our Lord Jesus gave the Church five servant ministry offices: apostles, prophets, evangelists, pastors, and teachers.[13] These are active ministries still available to the church today. The ministry gifts were given to strengthen the church, and this strength is just as necessary today. The Spirit of Jesus gave spiritual gifts to strengthen the church as it began, and they remain with us for the same purpose.[14] The spiritual gifts may include: words of wisdom, words of knowledge, faith for miracles, gifts for healing, prophetic gifts, discerning of spirits, teaching, preaching, speaking in spiritual language and tongues, and interpreting spiritual language and tongues. We must also include the Spirit's anointing for exegetical gifts, gifts of encouragement, singing in the spirit, generosity, service gifts, hospitality, gifted caregivers, anointed administrators, and spirit-inspired leaders of worship. All are awesome, powerful gifts for the work of the church, imparted to each one as the Spirit determines. By means of spiritual gifts Jesus' followers serve as His hand extended to those in need today; to prove His living, and active presence as the resurrected Christ.

But, too often, we are like the people of Malachi's time. We attempt to do the work of the church with useless fire—by means of our God-given common gifts and talents alone. Again, if our work is accomplished by means of common strength, we might as well shut the doors and go home.[15] Why are our weak efforts so detrimental? Because it is impossible to complete the Great Commission's work by human strength alone. We must turn away from using "useless fire" and do the work by means of the fire of the Spirit. The reason is simple:

---

13. Ephesians 4:11.
14. A more complete teaching on spiritual gifts is in the author's book, *Treasures of the Kingdom*.
15. This is not a reference to the doors of a physical church building.

What is impossible with man is possible with God.

(Luke 18:27)

Too often Christians either minimize or reject spiritual gifts that are given to strengthen the church. When we discard the gifts, we are left with common gifts and talents to do the job. But because we feel compelled to answer the mission's call, we refuse to wait and charge ahead with what little we have left.

As an example; one of the most useful spiritual gifts given to the church is the spiritual gift of prophecy. This gift serves to build up the church through encouragement, correction, admonishing, edifying, exposing sin,[16] and redirecting the church in the moment. Most of all, the spiritual gift of prophecy reveals the living, active presence of the resurrected Christ who is present with us to extend His hand to minister. This spiritual gift is the Spirit of Jesus who speaks to the church in the moment of crisis, in times of error, and calls us to repentance. This is a very important gift to strengthen the church, but we often reject the gift and replace it with "useless fires." Christian accountability groups and the shepherding movement are examples of useless fire in the church. When we reject the spiritual gift of prophecy the church becomes impoverished, leaving us with useless fire to do the work of the Great Commission.

Too many of the spiritual gifts given to enlighten the church have been minimized or rejected. Look at the gift of spiritual language as an example. This is one of the most misunderstood, maligned, and forbidden gifts of the Spirit of Christ. But it is an important utterance gift,[17] given to strengthen God's people.

The gift of tongues is more than speaking an unlearned language in times of worship, praying in the spirit, or singing in the spirit.[18] Its purpose is twofold. It is a sign for unbelievers to reveal Jesus' living presence and then open their eyes to see their need of Christ.

Tongues, then, are a sign, not for believers but for unbelievers;
prophecy, however, is not for unbelievers but for believers.

(1 Corinthians 14:22)

When this gift is ministered in the church, it must be translated into the common language of those gathered to worship. When translated, the ministry of tongues serves like the spiritual gift of prophecy. To reject this, or any

---

16. When sin is exposed by means of the spiritual gift of prophecy, this is not a finger pointing, name-calling, time for public humiliation. It comes across more as: "We have this sin among us, and this is a time for each of us to examine ourselves."
17. Prophecy, words of wisdom, words of knowledge, singing in the spirit, and speaking and interpreting unlearned languages are utterance gifts.
18. A further description of utterance gifts and spiritual language is found in *Treasures of the Kingdom*, page 118.

spiritual gift that is vital to the Church, causes a great loss and leaves us in an impoverished state.

God's people, the Church, are given powerful, effective spiritual gifts by the Holy Spirit of Jesus to accomplish an impossible task—the work of the Church and the Great Commission. Attempting to complete this work by means of God given common gifts is a great folly—it simply cannot be done. If this wisp of smoke is all we have left to fulfill our call, we might as well shut the doors and go home. But we are offered the fire of the Spirit to gift and empower us for the work, and we must not minimize or reject the Spirit's good gifts. There is no doubt that God will raise up an empowered people to complete the work of the Great Commission for the day of His return. The Apostle Paul speaks of God's faithfulness:

> *Being confident of this, that he who began a good work in you will carry it on to completion until the day of Christ Jesus.*
>
> (Philippians 1:6)

The Power and Effect of God's Holy Fire

Throughout the centuries of the old covenant, and now in the New Testament Church, fire has served many great purposes. This section leads us to see fire as a shield against those who are opposed to the Lord. We'll learn of God's purpose in the use of fire, and the effect of flames of fire. We'll see God's use of fire to establish covenant relationships, as a sign to get our attention so we will hear His still, small voice of love and mercy. This segment shows us a fire to cleanse and purify the saints, to reveal His presence, to protect His people, and to surround them with protective flames. We'll learn about the fire of the Spirit to empower God's people to fulfill their call, and to strengthen the saints to endure to the end.

The purpose of God's holy fire is evident, especially to establish covenants like He did with Abraham.[19] Fire is a visible manifestation of God's holy Presence. God's fiery presence ushered in the Abrahamic covenant, the Mosaic covenant, and finally a covenant for the New Testament Church.

We can comprehend God's holy fire and His nature in this encounter with Elijah.[20] God is a consuming fire, but He was not in the fire that appeared before Elijah. Instead, the Almighty spoke to the prophet in a still, small voice. God gave Elijah a task of restoring the people to covenant relationship. God gave Elijah signs and wonders as He did with Moses. Elijah's

---
19. Galatians 3:16.
20. 1 Kings 19:9–18.

signs were as powerful as wind that moves mountains, a force to shake the earth, and served as fearsome warnings. The omens were given to Elijah to awaken the people from spiritual wanderings. But God did not come against Israel in a destructive wind. God did not come to shake Israel with earthquakes to devastate them. God did not come with the fire of judgment upon Israel. No, God came with abundant mercy—in a still, small voice. All the warning signs and wonders Elijah performed dimmed in the light of God's grace and mercy, spoken in a still, small voice. On the mountain of the LORD, signs like thunder, earthquake, wind, and fire were given to make a way for the people to hear the still, small voice speak saving grace and mercy.

God desires to reveal His loving nature for us to see. Indeed, God is a consuming fire. He manifests His holy presence in fire. The Almighty commands the wind and the waves. He sends judgments of fire. And yet, God's still, small voice of mercy is greater than all the fire, wind, and earth-shaking signs and wonders. As we continue this chapter's study on fires of separation, keep in mind that God's abundant mercies are more awesome than His just and righteous judgments.

The fire of God's word cleanses us like a bar of soap that works to clean us from the inside out. The Holy Scriptures burn in our hearts to clean up our lives, and to purify us.

But who can endure the day of his coming? Who can stand when he appears? For he will be like a refiner's fire or a launderer's soap.

(Malachi 3:2)

Survival training offers an example of fire that purifies. Survivalists learn emergency techniques to use when no trained medical help is available. They are taught to sterilize a blade with a flame to cauterize a wound because fire works as a cleansing agent. Fire in the spiritual realm serves the same good purpose: to cleanse and purify. The fire of God's word is like a smelter's fire used to separate the dross from precious metals to refine and purify.

Remove the dross from the silver, and a silversmith can produce a vessel.

(Proverbs 25:4)

Purification is more important in the kingdom realm where Jesus' disciples are like precious stones made pure in the fires of affliction. The Apostle Peter alludes to the purification process:

> *These have come so that the proven genuineness of your faith–*
> *of greater worth than gold, which perishes even though refined by fire–*
> *may result in praise, glory and honor when Jesus Christ is revealed.*
>
> (1 Peter 1:7)

Because God's refining fire is often difficult and painful, we need to remind ourselves that this discipline is a true act of God's love lavished upon us. The refiner's fire in the realm of the kingdom of heaven is an awesome flame of love, because it purifies to prepare the bride of Christ for the Bridegroom. The Bridegroom's love is beautiful, and unmistakable in this love song from His beloved:

> *Place me like a seal over your heart, like a seal on your arm; for love is as strong as death, its jealousy unyielding as the grave. It burns like blazing fire, like a mighty flame.*
>
> (Song of Songs 8:6)

Fire of the Great I AM separates us from evil that would harm us, and purifies us so we may be separated to Christ. God's abundant love is the key to understand all of the Almighty's purpose and use of fire. For those who stand in opposition to the kingdom of heaven this is a consuming fire. This same fire acts through good deeds like pouring burning coals upon God's enemies.

> *If your enemy is hungry, feed him; if he is thirsty, give him something to drink. In doing this, you will heap burning coals on his head.*
>
> (Romans 12:20)

This is a terrifying fiery wrath that consumes the LORD's foes like chaff in a furnace.[21] Every fiery act of judgment brought against those who stand against Christ is an act of love toward those who are in Christ. Any one of us would demonstrate this same kind of protective love to protect our children and grandchildren from those who would dare harm them. And yet, God's love is even greater.

The fire of God's love toward the saints is awesome to behold. Because of His love, God tests us in the fire of affliction to perfect us.[22] He proves and strengthens our faith.[23] He gifts and empowers His disciples in the Spirit's fire.[24] His fire lights our way and guides us.[25] His fire burns in our hearts to

---

21. Psalm 89:46, Isaiah 33:14, Malachi 4:1
22. Malachi 3:1–5.
23. Romans 5:3–4, 1 Peter 4:12–19.
24. Matthew 3:11, Luke 3:16, Acts 1:8.
25. Isaiah 50:10–11.

compel us to speak out.[26] This holy fire drives us into the loving arms of our Lord and Savior.[27] God's holy fire shields and protects the family of God.[28]

Through awesome flames of fire, God established His covenants with Abraham and Moses, and at last, by fire, Christ brought the Church to life. Yehovah's laws are like the light of fire to reveal our sin and drive us to Christ for forgiveness and mercy. The fire of Christ's passion set the cornerstone of the church in place, and then the Church began in the flame of the Holy Spirit. After this fiery beginning, the disciples were sent out to do the work of the Great Commission.

This inferno continues its good work today. God is revealed by fire, and manifested in flames of fire, and the word of God is blaze to burn in our conscience to convict us of sin. The fire of the Spirit cleanses us, and also protects us like a wall of flames around us. We are tested in our faith to strengthen us to endure to the end. All of these good things God provides because of His abundant love for the sheep of His pasture.

Final Separation by Fire

Revelation is an awesome prophetic book with fire-breathing witnesses, lakes of fire, and fires from heaven that devour. But for the family of God, there is no cause for fear. Flames of fire have an integral part in God's final victory over death and the grave. This study section opens to us the Almighty's great victory with all enemies under His feet.[29] We will learn that His enemies are also our enemies. Together, by faith, we'll enter into Christ's fiery and final victory that destroys the cause of sorrow, tears, weeping, pain, and suffering.

He will wipe every tear from their eyes. There will be no more death, or mourning or crying or pain, for the old order of things has passed away.

(Revelation 21:4)

From Adam's fall in the beginning and to the end of time, God's purpose and plan has been to defeat death. The prophet Isaiah recorded what God spoke: that these powerful promises are fulfilled in the coming Messiah, our Lord and Savior, Jesus Christ.[30]

---

26. Psalm 39:3.
27. Zechariah 13:9.
28. Psalm 18:28–30, Isaiah 43:2, Zechariah 2:5.
29. Hebrews 10:13.
30. Luke 4:21.

He will swallow up death forever. The Sovereign Lord will wipe away the tears from all faces; he will remove his people's disgrace from all the earth. The Lord has spoken.

(Isaiah 25:8)

The Spirit of the Sovereign Lord is on me, because the Lord has anointed me to proclaim good news to the poor. He has sent me to bind up the brokenhearted, to proclaim freedom for the captives and release from darkness for the prisoners, to proclaim the year of the Lord's favor and the day of vengeance of our God, to comfort all who mourn, and provide for those who grieve in Zion— to bestow on them a crown of beauty instead of ashes, the oil of joy instead of mourning, and a garment of praise instead of a spirit of despair. They will be called oaks of righteousness, a planting of the Lord for the display of his splendor.

(Isaiah 61:1–3)

Think on the beauty of these words as Jesus spoke them—words of the Gospel's eternal promise. The work of the Gospel will be complete for all who come to saving faith, in God's final victory. The poor, the brokenhearted, those who despair, and the prisoners—all will be comforted. The ashes of their sorrows will be blown away, and like a bride adorned, we will display the Bridegroom's splendor.

The scene is very different for those who stand opposed to Christ, for those who enslave and impoverish people, for those who caused God's children to weep, and for all those who have caused so much pain and sorrow. Those who will not repent and turn from their violence will come to a fiery end.

They will be consigned to the fiery lake of burning sulfur. This is the second death.

(Revelation 21:8)

God's children will be forever separated from vicious and wicked people.

Then death and the grave were thrown into the lake of fire. This lake of fire is the second death. And anyone whose name was not recorded in the Book of Life was thrown into the lake of fire.

(Revelation 20:14–15 NLT)

There's a good reason for them to be condemned to the lake of fire. Nothing impure or harmful will ever enter into God's holy city, where we will dwell with Him, forever safe.

They will neither harm nor destroy on all my holy mountain,
for the earth will be filled with the knowledge of the Lord as the waters cover the sea.

(Isaiah 11:9)

God's great purpose and use of fire throughout all time is awesome to see. Creator God made the fiery sun to warm the earth. He created Orion's stars, the Pleiades cluster as luminaries in the sky. The Lord who made the sun and stars also provides fire for hearth and home, the light of a candle, and the fire of a lamp to light our way in the night. The Creator's lights separate day from night. The sun, moon and stars are signs for the seasons of the earth.[31]

God commanded Israel to offer sacrifices by fire for forgiveness of sin, and the smoke provided the pleasant aroma of worship.[32] The fire of the Law shows us our depravity and our need of Christ. In the fires of suffering, we see the futility of our human condition and we are driven to Christ to receive grace, mercy, and His healing touch. In Christ, the fire of the Holy Spirit is ignited in us as a guarantee of His saving grace. Jesus baptizes us in the fire of the Holy Spirit to anoint, gift, and empower us for Great Commission work. This work cannot be accomplished by means of common gifts and talents that are like useless fire. The fire of the Spirit refines, purifies, and protects us so we will have safe passage through the fire, and be separated to God in His glorious, fiery, eternal presence.

God established his covenants with Abraham, Moses, the nation of Israel, and finally the Church, each brought about through flames of fire—covenants to separate them as set apart to Christ the Messiah. God's word is like a fire, to light the flame of saving faith in our spirit, and then to work in us to purify, and cleanse us from every stain of sin. This fiery work separates God's people as His special possession.[33] With abundant love God wraps His arms around us. His Spirit burns in our hearts like a fire to separate us to Him, like a bride and groom who separate from mother and father to be together as one. In the fire of God's love, our faith is tested, our trust is strengthened; we are refined, made pure, and separated to prepare as a bride, inseparable from the Bridegroom. By means of God's holy fire, we are forever separated from any and all who would harm us or give cause for tears and sorrow. We are separated from death and the grave. The violent and unrepentant who stand opposed to God's kingdom are thrown into the lake of fire. All who are given a new name will dwell, safe and secure, in the glow of God's fiery presence for all eternity. A great victory is won, as the Apostle Paul declares:

---

31. Genesis 1:14–18.
32. Leviticus 4.
33. 1 Peter 2:9.

For I am convinced that neither death nor life, neither angels nor demons, neither the present nor the future, nor any powers, neither height nor depth, nor anything else in all creation, will be able to separate us from the love of God that is in Christ Jesus our Lord.

(Romans 8:38–39)

Chapter 7
Fire of Separation
Q & A

1. When we reject God's good gifts, what is the consequence?

2. God's word is like fire. For some, this is a consuming fire, and for others a cleansing fire. Why is the effect so different?

3. On the day of Pentecost in Acts chapter two, the people had two distinct responses to speaking in tongues. Explain why this happened.

4. The work of the Great Commission is not accomplished by means of mortal strength alone. Explain the significance of this truth.

My Journal Notes:

Chapter 8:
Body, Soul, and Spirit Work Together

Key Scriptures:

- "May God himself, the God of peace, sanctify you through and through. May your whole spirit, soul and body be kept blameless at the coming of our Lord Jesus Christ." (1 Thessalonians 5:23)
- "Do you not know that your bodies are members of Christ himself?" (1 Corinthians 6:15)

A clear distinction between what is holy and what is common is made in every chapter of this study guide. These separations are challenging because we are created beings with a body, soul, and spirit. We are three-part beings. Our created being has a body and spirit, and both ought to work together to fulfill God's good purpose. Meanwhile, the soul makes us a unique and special person. The separation taught here is not a separation of body from spirit, but a separation of body, soul, and spirit to Christ so we may know and accomplish our destiny and purpose.

In this study, we'll see God's clear and distinct function for each part of our being. The body serves a good and common purpose—to do our job and provide for our families. The body is also like a mortal seed that will be planted to spring up immortal in Christ. The soul gives each of us the ability to hear a different drummer, so to speak. It makes each of us one-of-a-kind. The third and eternal part of who we are is spirit. The wind of the Holy Spirit is breathed into each new creation in Christ to bring the seed into life forever.

Because the distinction between body, soul, and spirit is difficult, throughout religious history some have denigrated what is common in an attempt to elevate personal holiness. As an example, Gnostics believe that all physical matter is evil and only the spiritual is good. Religions like this deny what the body needs as they try to attain a higher spirituality. They practice extreme abstinence and ascetic living to transcend to a higher spiritual state. What they teach is destructive, and not Biblical. Their credos come from human reasoning and lead to a twisted exalting of the flesh—a false humility. They are a "look at me I'm so religious" kind of belief system. It's like putting a friend down to make ourselves look better only by comparison.

Because of a natural tendency to denigrate the body in an attempt to achieve greater spirituality, this chapter gives extra attention to the body's place in the work of the Great Commission. We must look at each part of our being to get a clear picture of the whole. It's a beautiful reality to see body, soul, and spirit come together to take part in what God plans to accomplish in us and through us.

The Body

Consider the importance of the physical body. Our LORD Jesus was made perfect in all holiness through suffering that included a physical body like ours.[1] Jesus, the last Adam,[2] was given a physical body to dwell among us and to suffer and die in our place, for our sin and for our salvation. By faith, He makes us holy even while in our physical, earthen bodies.

> *But now he has reconciled you by Christ's physical body through death to present you holy in his sight, without blemish and free from accusation.*
>
> (Colossians 1:22)

The Son of God became man with a body like ours and soiled His feet as He walked the dusty roads in the land of Israel. And then He willingly gave His physical body to be broken so we might be made whole in body, soul and spirit. Jesus' lifeblood was shed so that we might be forgiven, cleansed, washed, redeemed by the work of the cross, and made a working part in the body of Christ.

> *He [Jesus] was put to death in the body but made alive in the Spirit.*
>
> (1 Peter 3:18)

The Apostle Paul wrote in his letter to the Colossian church about suffering, like Jesus, in our physical body. Indeed, to be in Christ is a pathway of affliction until the final victory is won. The work of the cross is strengthened in sorrows. The travails of the Great Commission are worth every moment of painful trial and distress.

> *Now I rejoice in what I am suffering for you, and I fill up in my flesh what is still lacking in regard to Christ's afflictions, for the sake of his body, which is the church.*
>
> (Colossians 1:24)

Paul is not saying that the work of the cross of Jesus Christ is insufficient for washing away our sin and for our salvation. What he is saying is that in the sufferings of our physical body, we are conformed to Christ in His body, the Church. Our sufferings in the body for the cause of Christ are for the fulfillment of the work of the Church, which is the body of Christ. Paul invites us to enter Christ's sorrow:

---

1. Hebrews 2:10, 5:8.
2. The name Adam means "comes from the dust of the ground," אֲדָמָה *'ădâmâh*.

> *Join with me in suffering for the gospel, by the power of God.*
>
> (2 Timothy 1:8)

When we suffer, our LORD Jesus suffers, and He is familiar with suffering in a body like ours. And now the Spirit of Jesus is ever-present with us, especially in times of trouble. Consider that our bodies are like a perishable "seed" that dies when planted and then resurrected as imperishable. Until this earth-bound body is planted, we are called to overcome all the challenges the world throws at us; and this is only possible in Christ. This is taught throughout the book of Revelation with numerous references to "him who overcomes."[3] Paul's letters are a powerful expression of this truth:

> *So will it be with the resurrection of the dead. The body that is sown is perishable, it is raised imperishable; it is sown in dishonor, it is raised in glory; it is sown in weakness, it is raised in power; it is sown a natural body, it is raised a spiritual body.*
>
> *If there is a natural body, there is also a spiritual body. So it is written: "The first man Adam became a living being;" the last Adam, a life-giving spirit. The spiritual did not come first, but the natural, and after that the spiritual. The first man was of the dust of the earth; the second man is of heaven. As was the earthly man, so are those who are of the earth; and as is the heavenly man, so also are those who are of heaven. And just as we have borne the image of the earthly man, so shall we bear the image of the heavenly man.*
>
> *I declare to you, brothers and sisters, that flesh and blood cannot inherit the kingdom of God, nor does the perishable inherit the imperishable. Listen, I tell you a mystery: We will not all sleep, but we will all be changed–in a flash, in the twinkling of an eye, at the last trumpet. For the trumpet will sound, the dead will be raised imperishable, and we will be changed. For the perishable must clothe itself with the imperishable, and the mortal with immortality. When the perishable has been clothed with the imperishable, and the mortal with immortality, then the saying that is written will come true: "Death has been swallowed up in victory."*
>
> (1 Corinthians 15:42–54)

While we are still in this flesh and bone body, we are called to overcome so that we may inherit the kingdom of God and be victorious over the darkness of death. In this earthen body, we are planted like a seed to die in the ground and then spring up unto life eternal. First we are a perishable seed, and then in Christ we overcome what is wasting away to be clothed with what is forever and indestructible.

---

3. Revelation 2:7, 2:11, 2:17, 2:26, 3:5, 3:12, 3:21, 21:7 NKJV.

Because we are like a precious seed, we must not intentionally cause harm to our common flesh,[4] or despise God's temporal blessings in a futile attempt to promote false personal holiness. This is an important point. In Christ, there is no need for us to make our body suffer any more than it might naturally suffer through disease, age, or accident. There is sufficient suffering in the cause of Christ and His Church to have a full measure of misery in this life.

We don't cause harm to our bodies to accomplish the work of the Great Commission because we need a healthy body. We need to be strong physically to function as we serve to accomplish the work of the church. But keep in mind that the strength of our physical body has its limits.

> *For physical training is of some value, but godliness has value for all things, holding promise for both the present life and the life to come.*
> (1 Timothy 4:8)

God made us just as we are, and the unique person we are for His good purpose. Our body, mind, and personality are beautifully and wonderfully made. We're one of a kind, just as God intended. We are created unique to fulfill our God ordained destiny. It is good to accept ourselves just as God made us. Now take care of this good gift and our body will serve us well in this life, in accord with God's purpose and plan.

It's awesome to see body, soul, and spirit come together in prayer, praise, and worship before a holy God. Without a doubt, when we minister and serve before a holy God, we need this earthen vessel to keep us here on terra firma. We were given a unique body with special hands, mouth, and feet; each to do its part to complete the work of the kingdom. In fact, Christ is exalted in our body when we separate holy and common to worship, serve, and minister before the LORD Almighty.[5] The Apostle Paul instructs us to pray, to sing songs and hymns with our minds and with our spirit as we gather together in Jesus' name.

> *So what shall I do?*
> *I will pray with my spirit, but I will also pray with my understanding;*
> *I will sing with my spirit, but I will also sing with my understanding.*
> (1 Corinthians 14:15)

While here on earth, a body and mind are an important part of praise and worship. There are many ways to praise and worship before God Almighty, and these may well be described as various heights of worship. Yet, all forms of worship lifted up from the earth require us to be present in a body.

---

4. Even in fasting we must not harm our physical body. Fasting strengthens us in soul and spirit to overrule the "flesh," but must not harm the physical body.
5. Philippians 1:20.

What is gained if I am silenced, if I go down to the pit? Will the dust praise you? Will it proclaim your faithfulness?

(Psalm 30:9)

As an example: when we do the work given to us to provide for our families as unto the Lord, this is a form of praise.[6] When God's creation does what God created it to do, this too is a type of praise, and each requires a physical, material body of some kind. Praise is lifted up when the birds sing their songs, the flowers blossom, a baby cries her first cry, and when the sun and moon mark the seasons. Orion and Pleiades sing out with twinkling light, the tides roar, the clouds thunder and send rainfall and snow to water the earth—all these things do what God created them to do and each is received as praise.[7]

The birds' song is beautiful and the roar of the sea is awesome, but they are not the highest form of worship. The greatest and highest exaltation is to come into God's holy presence in reverence and awe to hear, receive, believe, and sing out words of eternal life. Lazarus' sister, Mary, showed us this kind of worship when she sat at Jesus' feet, treasuring every word He spoke.[8] At Jesus' transfiguration, God audibly spoke to call us to listen—a great means of worship.

A voice came from the cloud, saying, "This is my Son, whom I have chosen; listen to him."

(Luke 9:35)

This highest worship inspires greater service and ministry. From this pinnacle of worship, we are compelled to go out and speak what Jesus speaks, reach out and touch whom Jesus touches, and go where Jesus leads us. This is worship driven by the wind of the Spirit of Jesus who works in us and through us. This reverent worship flows from the hearts of those who stand in God's council and then speak out what God has spoken. We are strengthened to serve those to whom God is ministering in this kind of worship.

Singing out with Psalms, hymns, and spiritual songs to exalt the Lord Most High is a very excellent form of worship. In this hallowed, reverent worship, holy and common are separated—each for its own good purpose. When common hands are lifted up to heaven in praise and worship, the Lord honors them as holy. When the presence of a holy God enters His temple, the noises of the world are silenced to make way for greater, higher, and abundant worship to all those who gather in Jesus' name.

---

6. Colossians 3:23.
7. Psalm 148.
8. Luke 10:39.

The Lord is in his holy temple; let all the earth be silent before him.

(Habakkuk 2:20)

Both what is common and what is holy are excellent for praise and worship before a holy God. Each is good in its place, and we must not diminish either. A feathered body is necessary for birds to sing and a furry one is needed for the lion that roars. This body covered with skin that God gave us has a part in our kingdom service and its best work is done when working together with a redeemed soul and spirit. Each has its place and each serves its good purpose. When we lift up our hands in a gathering of believers, this alone is not worship. But when we set our hearts and minds on our Father, and our spirits are lifted in the Spirit to raise holy hands, our body and spirit come together in worship.

A beautiful example of this separation is given to us in the account of Jesus calming the storm on the Sea of Galilee.[9] This Gospel account makes clear Jesus' humanity and His deity. Humanity and deity, of course, are not the same, but they came together in Jesus. Exhaustion took over His human body and the storm couldn't wake him. He slept through it on a cushion in the stern of the rocking boat. His disciples feared for their lives and shook Him awake. Jesus rose up and spoke to the wind and the waves and the waters of Galilee became calm and still. Jesus, the man, became physically exhausted. Jesus, Immanuel, spoke the words of God with His mouth and calmed the storm.

He stilled the storm to a whisper; the waves of the sea were hushed.

(Psalm 107:29)

Christians are both earthbound beings (temporarily) and spiritual beings (forever). We get exhausted and the Lord strengthens us in body and spirit to do His work and fulfill His call. How does this principle apply to our daily lives and to our Christian service? When we pray to the Lord, we pray with our minds and we pray with our spirit. When we sing out to the Lord, we sing with our mind and sing in the spirit. When we minister in our spiritual gift to those in need, we minister in the spirit, by means of the Holy Spirit. Our flesh-and-bone hands serve as the hands of Jesus by means of the Spirit of Christ. When we play the flute to accompany a time of worship, we play with practiced skill, and the powerful eternal effect comes by means of the gift and power of the Spirit at work in us and through us. When we mop the kitchen floor, we use the physical strength God has given us to wring out the mop, and we clean the floors as unto the Lord—with a heart that overflows with wor-

---

9. Luke 8:22–25.

shipful service. We use the God-given gift of self-discipline to effectively study God's word so that we will grow spiritually, and our spirit will be opened to understand the truth of the Scriptures by the power of the Spirit of Christ.

It is good in every way for those who are teachers and preachers of God's word to be educated and trained in the disciplines of studying the Scriptures. They study hermeneutics so they can master the skills to prepare themselves to present the truths of Scripture. And yet, when they finally get their sheepskin from the university, it should be counted as nothing. The Apostle Paul was highly educated under Gamaliel, one of the master teachers of the Law. He was a Hebrew of Hebrews; from the tribe of Benjamin—a great family heritage. But he counted it all as nothing.

But whatever were gains to me I now consider loss for the sake of Christ. What is more, I consider everything a loss because of the surpassing worth of knowing Christ Jesus my Lord for whose sake I have lost all things. I consider them garbage, that I may gain Christ and be found in him, not having a righteousness of my own that comes from the law, but that which is through faith in Christ—the righteousness that comes from God on the basis of faith.

(Philippians 3:7–9)

All the preparation and training we receive is good and valuable, but compared to the power, strength, and anointing of the Spirit of Jesus, it is nothing; and should be counted as nothing. This human body has an important part in worship, service, and ministry, but should be considered of little value to accomplish what is of eternal value.

The Soul

The other part of our person that God created in His image is the soul. What part does a person's soul play in our work, service, and ministry? The soul gives our worship, our ministry, and service it's unique and special character. Each person's worship and service will be distinct, and God delights in our uniqueness.

For example, when we read the Old Testament prophets, we see that even though they spoke and wrote what they heard God speaking, each one expressed the oracles of God in a unique and special way. God will never use automatons with pre-recorded messages. He uses people who have special and unique personalities who can speak out His message in a way only they can speak. Their distinctive expressions make receiving it possible for unique ears that might only hear their special voice. Isaiah wrote what he heard the Almighty speaking with poetic words—often metaphorically. Jeremiah wrote on the scrolls in mournful tones, as if with weeping. David's unique soul expressed his yearning for the Lord with musical Psalms.

> *As the deer pants for streams of water, so my soul pants for you, my God.*
> *My soul thirsts for God, for the living God. When can I go and meet with God?*
>
> (Psalm 42:1–2)

Our soul's special way of doing things is for a good purpose. Because every person hears, reacts, and responds in a different way, each of us needs a unique messenger to speak out the Good News Gospel. There are some people who will only hear the truth of God's saving grace in the unique way one person proclaims it. There are specific people who may not understand what one person says, but will respond to the way another says it. This is a soul-to-soul connection that is the work of the Spirit of Jesus.

The Spirit

The third part of who we are is spirit. This is the part of our being that lights up when we are made a new creation in Christ. Our spirit is the part of us that can connect with God's Spirit in worship, praise, thanksgiving, and in the ministries of the church. Our spirit has spiritual ears to know the Good Shepherd's voice and to hear the Spirit of Christ speak. Our spirit has spiritual eyes to see into what cannot be seen with our natural eyes—by means of the Spirit of Jesus. The Spirit of Creator God breathed His wind into Adam to make him live as a spiritual being with understanding and a voice. In the same way, the wind of a person's spirit comes together with the Spirit's breath, the wind of the Almighty, to open our hearts and minds to understand spiritual things.[10] In the spirit, we gain knowledge that no one could ever teach us apart from the help of the Holy Spirit. A new-born Christian's spirit confirms their adoption as a son or daughter of our heavenly Father.

> *The Spirit himself testifies with our spirit that we are God's children.*
>
> (Romans 8:16)

Our spirit strengthens us in times of trouble and when our body grows old and weak.[11] The spirit part of a person is critical for life, because when it departs and ascends to Christ, the body no longer sustains life.[12] Most important of all, a person's spirit and soul are eternal. This is the forever part of us that will be joined with our immortal body to dwell with the Bridegroom for eternity.

---

10. Proverbs 20:27.
11. 1 Thessalonians 5:23.
12. Ecclesiastes 12:7, James 2:26.

As we separate what is holy from what is common, it becomes clear that body, soul, and spirit work together. We must not limit ourselves to what is mortal and common as we come into the highest form of worshipful service and ministries before a holy God.

Jacob's life story is an illustration of how body, soul, and spirit work together. He became the father of the twelve patriarchs of the tribes of God's chosen nation. He began his life journey to this position of honor as a young man who had to run for his life after he stole his brother's birthright. Then, as he camped for the night with only a rock for a pillow, he saw angels descend from God's presence and ascend again to heaven on a ladder. This was an awesome revelation of a holy God and the glory and majesty of the kingdom of heaven.

Twenty-one years later, the angel of God's presence appeared to Jacob and he wrestled with the angel until daybreak. The angel gave Jacob a new name, Israel, because he struggled with God and with men and overcame. As He fulfilled His promise, God displayed His faithfulness, mercy, and majesty. Jacob prevailed with the angel of the LORD, but not by human strength. In the strength of his spirit he wrestled and held the angel until he received a blessing. Then the angel struck Jacob's hip and sent him on his way, but with a limp. This limp may well have been to remind him and all his progeny of our human fallibility.

The man, Jacob, didn't have the power to help God fulfill His promise that the younger son would serve the eldest son. But because he tried to make it happen on his own, he had to flee from his brother's murderous anger. It was in his spirit, empowered in the Spirit, that he wrestled with God's holy angel and prevailed.

The Apostle Paul "was caught up to paradise and heard inexpressible things, things that no one is permitted to tell."[13] And, like Jacob, "because of these surpassingly great revelations,"[14] Paul was given a "thorn in [his] flesh" to keep him from becoming conceited. The thorn always reminded him of his human weaknesses that might hinder the work of the spirit that could only be accomplished by means of the Spirit of Christ.

In all that God has called us to do, while this common body is a necessary part of the work, it is not the primary element in kingdom work. The common flesh and its achievements must be counted as nothing, for they cannot accomplish God's holy purpose. Our hands, our feet, and our minds are needed for service and ministry. But what is common cannot achieve the immeasurable work of the kingdom of heaven with eternal effect.

---

13. 2 Corinthians 12:4.
14. 2 Corinthians 12:7.

The conclusion is obvious: God has given us a human body and mortal abilities, and this gift of human strength is good in its place. We must take good care of the body to keep it healthy and strong for the common good, and for the work of the kingdom of heaven. We must not denigrate our human strength because we cannot accomplish the work God has appointed for each of us here on earth without it.

Our soul gives the kingdom work we do its unique and special essence. No one else can accomplish the work we are called to do in the way that only we can do it. The soul makes our work unique in order to reach others in a way no one else can.

Our spirit keeps us connected to the Spirit of a holy God. In the spirit, we may stand in God's council. In the spirit, we bow in God's holy presence to worship. In the spirit, we are given the power and strength to minister and serve, to fulfill our call in the impossible work of the church, the kingdom of heaven, and the Great Commission.

What is impossible with man is possible with God.

(Luke 18:27)

Chapter 8
Body, Soul, and Spirit Work Together
Q & A

1. Describe how body, soul, and spirit come together in a gathering of prayer, praise, and worship.

2. What is the highest form of worship? What makes it far above every means of exaltation?

3. What is the value of achievements like a university degree, a great resume, and an honored place in this life?

My Journal Notes:

Chapter 9:
Gates and Walls of Separation

Key Scriptures:

- "Lift up your heads, you gates; lift them up, you ancient doors, that the King of glory may come in." (Psalm 24:9)
- "'And I myself will be a wall of fire around it,' declares the Lord, 'and I will be its glory within.'" (Zechariah 2:5)

Gates and walls of every kind are found throughout the Scriptures. The course of history often changed when armies crossed the mountains, built siege ramps against a city's walls, or breached its gates. In ancient times, walls were built around a city to protect the inhabitants from warrior kings who came to plunder. Kings were seated to judge their subjects in the gateways of ancient hamlets. Provisions from nearby farms entered through the village gates. The town elders held court to mete out justice and settle disputes at these busy intersections.[1] A city's gates and walls served a good and common purpose.

Gates and walls in God's kingdom serve a holy purpose. As an example, the builders of the Old Testament temple of worship constructed it according to God's plan with gates and walls to separate the holy from what was common.

In the Scriptures, different instruments were used to separate: a shepherd's staff, a ruler's rod, a warrior's sword, and a king's scepter. God's purposes for separations are many: to protect, to own, to have, and to hold. Even today, wedding ceremonies separate two people from their parents and join them together as one in a new family. It's a great insight to see the beauty and purpose of God's great separations. Walls separate the Father's children from the darkness of sin and the tentacles of evil. Through the Gate, we enter into the light of Christ to enjoy fellowship with our heavenly Father.

In this chapter, we will see God's sovereignty at work like a wall to protect those He adopts as His children. We will step through the Gate of renewal—Christ Jesus. We will be set free from the snares of sin inside a wall called Freedom. The righteousness of Christ will be credited to us when we, by faith, are brought through the gate of justification. At last, in the shelter of the wall that separates us, we will no longer be weighed down by sin's condemnation and guilt. We will discover God's good purpose for walls to separate and gates for us to enter.

---

1. Proverbs 31:23.

A Gate Opened

In Jesus' parable of the wedding banquet, He drew a word picture as He told about a great king who prepared a celebration for his son. Take a moment to press into the crowd, sit in the grassy meadow, and listen to Jesus teach.

> *Jesus spoke to them again in parables, saying: "The kingdom of heaven is like a king who prepared a wedding banquet for his son. He sent his servants to those who had been invited to the banquet to tell them to come, but they refused to come.*
>
> *"Then he sent some more servants and said, 'Tell those who have been invited that I have prepared my dinner: My oxen and fattened cattle have been butchered, and everything is ready. Come to the wedding banquet.'*
>
> *"But they paid no attention and went off—one to his field, another to his business. The rest seized his servants, mistreated them and killed them. The king was enraged. He sent his army and destroyed those murderers and burned their city.*
>
> *"Then he said to his servants, 'The wedding banquet is ready, but those I invited did not deserve to come. So go to the street corners and invite to the banquet anyone you find.' So the servants went out into the streets and gathered all the people they could find, the bad as well as the good, and the wedding hall was filled with guests.*
>
> *"But when the king came in to see the guests, he noticed a man there who was not wearing wedding clothes. He asked, 'How did you get in here without wedding clothes, friend?' The man was speechless.*
>
> *"Then the king told the attendants, 'Tie him hand and foot, and throw him outside, into the darkness, where there will be weeping and gnashing of teeth.'*
>
> *"For many are invited, but few are chosen."*
>
> (Matthew 22:1–14)

Today, the King of kings is still sending out invitations for everyone, inviting them to the Son's wedding banquet. The panhandler outside the grocery store gets an invitation. The homeless man sleeping under the bridge receives an invitation. Governors, mayors, senators, and government officials are sent invitations. Even lawyers and IRS agents are invited to this great celebration.

But of all the people who are invited, only a few will show up at the garden gate for the wedding celebration. These few come, not because they just decided to, but because the invitation touched their hearts to create a desire to come. It's like the invitation switched on a light deep inside of them, and their hearts compelled them to come to the wedding banquet.

The no-shows were too busy. Other obligations and schedule conflicts kept them away. Some despised the invitation, and retorted: "So we're supposed to care about the Son's wedding banquet?"

For those whose hearts compelled them to celebrate with the king, when entering the garden gate, they were given a new wedding garment; they were wrapped in a robe made for the occasion. If anyone tried to sneak in without the wedding garment offered, no matter how fine the clothes they wore, they would be bound and thrown out into the darkness. But all those with a wedding robe enjoyed a great festive celebration. They sang, danced, and feasted with the King's Son in a grand wedding celebration. Indeed, by entering this gate, a few were separated from all those who were invited but didn't have time for such frivolity. Only a few would be delighted to hear the King's words:

Enter into the joy of your master.

(Matthew 25:23 ESV)

Sovereign Election: A Wall

I will have mercy on whom I have mercy,
and I will have compassion on whom I have compassion.

(Romans 9:15)

From the beginning of time, God knew our name. He knew our heart, and He determined our destiny. He chose us, and He called us out of darkness—He called each of us by name. Even before we were conceived, many thousands of years before we were brought into this world, God knew our name and loved us.

Because of His love for us, God called us His own, and gave each of us a purpose—a work to accomplish. As He created all the heavens and the earth, He included us in His master plan. It's as if the Creator drew out a road map for all time from beginning to end. At one intersection of time, He saw us and made a note of our name at the crossroads, saying; "I need her right here to accomplish an important job in my plan." Above all else, because of His mercy and grace, He wrote our name in the Book of Life many generations before we were born. We would not be like the thief who attempts to climb over the wall of sovereign election to get in by his own doing.

In God's great act of love, He chose each one who would be His child and gave us a new family name. He separated us from the darkness of this world, just as sheep are kept safe inside the walls of the sheepfold from prowling predators in the night. In God's abundant love, we are lifted up to bring glory and honor to our heavenly Father.

But you are a chosen people, a royal priesthood, a holy nation, God's special possession, that you may declare the praises of him who called you out of darkness into his wonderful light.

(1 Peter 2:9)

Regeneration: A Gate

If you violated the law and were found guilty of violent crimes against humanity, the judge would slam his gavel down and declare a death sentence. Then you would be bound in a cold, hard electric chair with your wrists shackled to the arms. You would watch as the executioner's hand takes hold of the switch. Then you might clench your teeth and close your eyes tight, wondering what comes after dying.

But then you hear the door to the execution chamber swing open. You blink your eyes as a man walks in, unshackles your hands, helps you out of the chair, and sits down in your place. You're guilty as hell and you know it, but this man takes your place in the chair and willingly dies in your place, for what you did wrong, for your great offenses, because you were condemned to die. The guards take you to the prison gate; it's opened and you are set free. But more than set free—no longer condemned, you have a change of heart; you are given a new name, and a job to do.

Because through Christ Jesus the law of the Spirit who gives life has set you free from the law of sin and death. For what the law was powerless to do because it was weakened by the flesh, God did by sending his own Son in the likeness of sinful flesh to be a sin offering. And so he condemned sin in the flesh, in order that the righteous requirement of the law might be fully met in us, who do not live according to the flesh but according to the Spirit.

(Romans 8:2–4)

In one moment, you were as good as a dead man in the electric chair, and in the next you were set free—free from the penalty of death. As you enter through this gate, you are separated from the curse of death, and you step into the light of life—forever.

Freedom from Sin: A Wall

Have you ever been caught up in a self-destructive pattern of behavior, but just can't make yourself stop? It's like what you do is ingrained in your genes, and there is nothing you can do to change your behavior. What you do is habitual, and it has a stranglehold on your whole life. Like chains on your wrists, or a ball and chain around your neck, you're dragged down again and again. If you're told to stop, you want to do it even more than before. This is the power of sin in your life. Vices become addictive and bind us as if with chains.

The evil deeds of a wicked man [woman] ensnare him; the cords of his sin hold him fast.

(Proverbs 5:22)

The apostle Paul talks us through the strange power of sinful desires. The following verse would leave us in a helpless state if Paul didn't show us a way out and give us the way of hope. "But who will rescue me?" "Who has the power to release me from the chains of death?"

So I find this law at work: Although I want to do good, evil is right there with me. For in my inner being I delight in God's law; but I see another law at work in me, waging war against the law of my mind and making me a prisoner of the law of sin at work within me. What a wretched man I am! Who will rescue me from this body that is subject to death? Thanks be to God, who delivers me through Jesus Christ our Lord!

(Romans 7:21–25)

This wall separates us, and then protects us from the power of evil, the force of sin, the snares of our sinful nature, and death that results from sin. Inside this wall, we find healing from the wounds of sin and a new freedom in Christ.

Justification by Faith: A Gate

*Therefore, since we have been justified through faith,
we have peace with God through our Lord Jesus Christ.*

(Romans 5:1)

The gift of faith to believe in the resurrected Christ as LORD and Savior is the greatest gift of all time—a gift with eternal value. When we receive this gift, the greatest miracle happens: we are made a new creation in Christ Jesus. Saving faith is not like a strike of lightning out of nowhere, but comes by hearing God's Word with not only our ears, but our heart, soul, and spirit. God's holy Word permeates our hearing, changes our heart, sparks faith in us, and drives out the darkness of sin. By faith we are made right before Creator God, justified and at peace in our LORD, Jesus Christ.

As we are led by the Good Shepherd to step through this gate, we are brought into peace with a holy God, forgiven, washed clean, and sealed by the Holy Spirit so we may stand in the presence of God Almighty. We are separated and released from sin's deadly grasp.

Separation from Guilt: A Wall

Therefore, there is now no condemnation for those who are in Christ Jesus.

(Romans 8:1)

God's kindness is intended to lead you to repentance.

(Romans 2:4)

Romans chapter eight is one of the richest treasure-troves of life-giving words in the Bible. The freedom set before us in these words written by the Apostle Paul is not only miraculous, but also practical and useful in daily life.

My grandmother often felt burdened with self-condemnation. She bore the weight of guilt for no good reason. I think she felt guilty about feeling guilty. The good LORD gave her a great gift to lift this burden of guilt. She memorized Romans chapter eight. It's as if I can still hear her quietly whisper: "There is therefore now no condemnation for those who are in Christ Jesus."[2]

God's word declares that we are free from the condemnation of the Law and given freedom in Christ. Our LORD and Savior gives us freedom from guilt that would weigh us down. With all kindness and gentleness, the Good Shepherd leads us into the sheepfold to separate us from self-condemnation, and from condemnation that comes from the burden of the Law. We are washed in the blood of the Lamb and wrapped in Jesus' robe of righteousness.

Blessed are those who wash their robes,
that they may have the right to the tree of life and may go through the gates into the city.

(Revelation 22:14)

Secure Walls with Beautiful Gates

Walls and gates are effective and purposeful separators. God began to separate on the first day of creation, and He continues to separate in the world today. The Gate is now open to all those who will come to the great wedding feast. A wall of mercy and compassion protects God's adopted children from the deceitfulness of darkness. As we enter the gate of regeneration, we are made a new creation in Christ. The wall of freedom separates us from the power of sin and breaks the chains of addiction that once held us in their grip. When, by faith, we enter the beautiful gate called Justification, all the good that Christ has done is credited to us, and God sees us as pure and innocent. The LORD God provides a wall that separates us from the guilt of

---

2. Romans 8:1.

our sin. Surrounded by this wall, we no longer need to feel the condemnation of sin. We are invited to enter by this beautiful Gate and separate ourselves in Christ. We find protection in His holiness and righteousness. God's holy word calls out to each of us to be separated from the world and He takes His adopted, as sons and daughters, into His loving arms to be children of the Most High God. Jesus offered up His body as a sacrifice to redeem us and break the chains of sin, to purify us, and to separate unto Himself a people to call His own, who delight in righteousness.[3] God's great purpose for the gates and walls He provides is to make us forever inseparable from Christ.

Chapter 9
Gates and Walls of Separation
Q & A

1. What good purposes do gates and walls serve in God's eternal plan?

2. How have the Gospel's "gates" and "walls" affected you in your Christian life and service?

3. What is the greatest of all miracles?

---

3. Titus 2:13–14.

My Journal Notes:

Chapter 10:
The Benefits of Separation

Key Scriptures:

- "Therefore, 'Come out from them and be separate, says the Lord. Touch no unclean thing, and I will receive you.'" (2 Corinthians 6:17)

- "Depart, depart, go out from there! Touch no unclean thing! Come out from it and be pure, you who carry the articles of the Lord's house. But you will not leave in haste or go in flight; for the Lord will go before you, the God of Israel will be your rear guard." (Isaiah 52:11–12)

The value gained from separating holy from common is still relevant for the modern-day church. In this chapter, we'll explore how God's people come into His strength that is necessary for the work of the Great Commission. We'll look back to the work of godly American forefathers that still serves to instruct us. Also, the words of the Old Testament prophets offer valuable lessons for us.

Real-life examples show us what we gain as we separate ourselves to Christ. In this study, we'll also learn about the great risk when we do not keep holy and common separate. It's important to make clear that keeping holy and common separate is not the same as separating holy from what is unclean. This is an important distinction because when we use what is common in place of what is holy, it is insufficient for God's purpose. As an example: fire is a good and common thing when it burns in the fireplace to warm the home. But look what happened when Aaron's sons Nadab and Abihu used common fire in place of holy fire from the altar. They were consumed by the fire of Yehovah's holy presence.[1] This serves as a warning to all who serve to accomplish the work of the Great Commission. We must not use our God-given common talents in place of the anointing, gifting, and empowering of the Holy Spirit. When we try to use common abilities to do the work of the Church, these good skills are unclean for the Spirit's holy purpose.

This separation is difficult because at times, in the work of God's kingdom, we are called to begin the work in the strength we have.[2] It's as if we take the first stride as a step of faith, only to find that our common strengths are inadequate for the task. Then, in the anointing of the Holy Spirit, we are empowered to accomplish what is otherwise impossible.

---

1. Leviticus 10:1–3.
2. Judges 6:14.

The void in our understanding compels us to be faithful and dig into God's word to learn these truths. Separation opens doors to bring us in so we may be protected from human infirmities, impurities, and from the darkness of a lost and dying world. We are brought into Christ to be made part of the whole body of Christ.

The founding fathers of the American system of government understood the societal benefits of keeping holy and common separate. To accomplish this, they inaugurated a government that could not establish any religion. They regarded the church as holy and the state as common. They saw both as good in their place, and believed that God established both. Our nation's founders knew the church could not do the work of civil governance, and the state should not attempt to do the work of the church. Our founders understood that the power of civil authority, when mixed with the sway of the church, eventually leads to conflict in freedom to worship and religious liberties.

While both holy and common are under God's sovereign rule, they are not interchangeable. One great advantage of separation is a purity of purpose. When church and state are blended in purpose, each one empowering the other, neither will function as the Creator intended. As an example, when the state begins to establish and impose values and morality, this creates conflict with the church. The true basis of moral standards is eroded. When the state redefines marriage in a way that conflicts with the church, a wall is necessary to resolve this clash of values. The Old Testament prophet Ezekiel shows us the beauty of this separation. Take a few steps back and observe what the Almighty reveals in Ezekiel's vision.

> *So he measured the area on all four sides. It had a wall around it, five hundred cubits long and five hundred cubits wide, to separate the holy from the common.*
>
> (Ezekiel 42:20)

In Ezekiel chapter four, the angel measured the temple with great detail. The "man whose appearance was like bronze"[3] measured the temple with the rod. This illustrates for us God's great purpose and the benefits of the holy separated from what is common. The test of the measuring rod confirmed that the temple was holy, prepared by God's design for His holy presence. And then an awesome miracle took place.

> *Then the man brought me to the gate facing east,*
> *and I saw the glory of the God of Israel coming from the east.*
>
> (Ezekiel 43:1–2)

---

3. Ezekiel 40:3.

This truth ought to hit us like a tsunami. When we connect the two Scriptures in sequence, it's like turning on all the stadium's flood lights. When the measurements were completed, God's glory returned to the temple. It's easy to miss the dynamics of what happened here. The "man whose appearance was like bronze" held a linen cord and a measuring rod in his hand. With them he measured the temple to be sure it was prepared, ready for God's presence—holy and in accord with God's plan. The temple design separated the holy from the common and the measurements proved it to be true. The temple was completely prepared for God's holy presence.

We too, as temples of the Holy Spirit, are to measure ourselves[4] and separate what is holy from what is common. When we do this, the effect is powerful beyond description. Ezekiel became a witness to this powerful effect when he was brought to the city gate facing east and shown the glory of the LORD returning to the temple.

For all who are called to serve as priests in God's kingdom, this truth will change our lives, our church, and the world around us. Listen to this! It's important to hear this truth: When what is holy was separated from the common, God's glory returned to the temple. Too many Christian churches today have not separated holy from common, and we are an impoverished people—spiritual paupers. What we are missing is God in all His holiness, majesty, and glory. The Great I AM waits like a mighty flood for us to separate what is common from what is holy.

This holds great importance for God's people today. All who are called by the name of Christ are temples of the Holy Spirit. But all too often, we use what God has given to men and women for the common good in a weak and futile attempt to accomplish the work of God's eternal kingdom. Our common talents are unclean for God's holy purpose. It cannot be said too often: the work of the church and the call of the Great Commission, in this day, cannot be accomplished by means of what is common. A person who only has a natural or common gift to teach, for instance, is not the person who is best equipped to teach spiritual truths with eternal effect. A soul is not won by means of taught skills, accurate historical accounts, or good information. We are fallible people who tend to fall back into common mode. We must constantly remind ourselves that God will not yield His glory to what is common.[5]

Think about it. Test this in the whole of Scripture to prove or refute what is taught here. Prayerfully meditate on this truth and you will see. The great benefit of separating holy from common is that God's glory will return to

---

4. 2 Corinthians 13:5.
5. Isaiah 42:8.

your temple in increasing measure. God can use you in a powerful and effective way as His instrument to accomplish all He has purposed and planned. This separation prepares your temple for an increased measure of the Holy Spirit's gifts and power. You will become empowered to advance the cause of Christ and the kingdom of heaven.

Beyond doubt, God is at work through Christians today. His hand is upon His people to accomplish what He has called us to do. But we limit the power and work of the Spirit of Jesus when we attempt to accomplish this good work in our common strength. This final leg of the Great Commission work requires the strength and power of the Spirit of Jesus in greater measure to gift and empower His people for works of service and ministry. The Apostle Paul's words encourage us to be strong in Christ's strength:

To this end I strenuously contend with all the energy Christ so powerfully works in me.

(Colossians 1:29)

There is a great work to be finished—Great Commission work given to us as Jesus ascended into heaven. To complete this work, we must separate what is holy from what is common to fulfill our call in the power of the Spirit of Jesus.

One of the great benefits of gazing into the fullness of Christ, the Word, is that it's like seeing the flashes and reflections of a multi-faceted diamond. But when we, as finite human beings, focus our attentions, our belief systems, and our theology on just a few facets of truth, we miss much of the value and the splendor of the many facets revealed in the Scriptures. When we narrow our focus, it causes erroneous thinking and skewed meditations. Our limited view causes us to miss the fullness of God's benefits—the beauty, power, and majesty of our Redeemer, Jesus Christ. This limited viewpoint keeps us from the fullness of Christ. For those who desire to dwell in the full light and presence of holiness we ought to be hungry and thirsty, and search for all God has given us for our good.

Even more than this, when we continue to call what is common "holy," and exalt what is common as if it is holy, we are using unclean, common fire in place of what is holy. This unclean fire eventually will eventually draw us into an idolatry of self. When we do this, whether in ignorance or arrogance, we enter into false worship in a most offensive and depraved manner.

Because the concept of separating two good things, holy and common, is so unfamiliar to today's Christian, an example may be helpful. Church leaders often tell a public schoolteacher that they have a spiritual gift to teach, and then ask them to teach Sunday school. If a Christian is a good public speaker, they're told, "You should be a preacher." When a person is loving, compassionate, and caring toward those around them, they're told: "You have a pastor's heart. You should be a pastor." But the work of a teacher, a speaker, and a caregiver in the common realm is not the work of a teacher, preacher, or pastor in the church.

This next example helps us understand the ridiculous nature of mixing holy and common with regard to spiritual gifts. Many churches have firefighters who attend. Their work is to put out fires and rescue people during some very traumatic incidents. If a firefighter has a common gift for rescue, shouldn't she also be good at putting out "fires" in the church caused by friction between members? No! Of course not. To extinguish flames in a house fire with fire trucks, ladders, and fire hoses is different from putting out "fires" caused by friction in the church. It's quite obvious that the work of Christian discipline is a spiritual matter—a holy work.

In the same way, the work of teacher, healer, preacher, pastor, or evangelist is unique to the kingdom of heaven. It isn't automatic for a doctor who practices medicine to have the spiritual gift of healing. The practice of medicine is his God given common gift brought to reality through years of education and experience. It isn't inevitable for a woman who is a gifted speaker to have a spiritual gift for preaching. A teacher who is gifted to teach math, history, or English is not guaranteed to have a spiritual gift to teach truths of the kingdom of heaven for eternal benefit.

We are called to separate the common from what is holy, because when we attempt to do the work of the kingdom by means of what is common, we take away from God's glory. When we attempt to serve by means of our own resources, we reduce ourselves to ministry by our own means, in our own strength, and we will be left with little more than wood, hay, and stubble.

If anyone builds on this foundation using gold, silver, costly stones, wood, hay or straw, their work will be shown for what it is, because the Day will bring it to light. It will be revealed with fire, and the fire will test the quality of each person's work. If what has been built survives, the builder will receive a reward. If it is burned up, the builder will suffer loss but yet will be saved–
even though only as one escaping through the flames

(1 Corinthians 3:12–15)

Our faith is strengthened when we are separated into Christ. We become like refined, precious metal that passes through a purifying fire. This truth becomes evident in the interaction between Martha and Jesus. When Martha spoke to Jesus about her brother, Lazarus, who laid dead in his grave, Jesus redirected her focus and then asked a pertinent question:

> *I am the resurrection and the life. The one who believes in me will live, even though they die; and whoever lives by believing in me will never die. Do you believe this?*
>
> (John 11:25–26)

When Martha tearfully confronted Jesus about her brother's death, Jesus didn't ask her if she believed that Lazarus would be raised from the dead. Instead, He refocused her faith on the One who is the Resurrection and the Life. This is an important separation for us as well. We are often confronted with this same test of trust. Do we have faith to believe we will receive what we ask for, or is our faith in the Giver of the Gift? If our faith focuses on what we desire; our faith is shakable. But if our faith is in God who is all sufficient, this is an uncommon faith and an unshakable faith. Our faith must not be fixed on what we hope to receive in answer to our prayers, but instead its object must be our Lord, God. Our faith must be greater than to receive what we ask. Our trust is fixed on the heavenly Father, God who Provides.

This is faith that separates what is holy from what is common, and in this there is great benefit—a faith that will not be shaken. The eyes of true faith look upon what is unseen and eternal, not upon what is only of temporal value—and this faith is unshakable. This faith carries us into the fullness of Christ.

May the Lord call us to repentance so that we may walk in the light of Christ. The fruit of repentance is to walk in spiritual abundance, and to gain the fullness of Christ in all His glory. God's people are called to turn away from serving in mortal strength alone. We serve in the power of the Name, separating what is holy from what is common to accomplish Great Commission work. We must count as nothing the work we might accomplish in our own strength. We turn away from this to minister in the power and strength of the Spirit. This is separation with great purpose; to reveal the living, active presence of Jesus Christ. It's better than getting a second wind to finish a marathon. It's the second wind of the Spirit to finish the Great Commission marathon. Those who run in their own strength will be left in the dust.

> *Even youths grow tired and weary, and young men stumble and fall; but those who hope in the Lord will renew their strength. They will soar on wings like eagles; they will run and not grow weary, they will walk and not be faint.*
>
> (Isaiah 40:30–31)

My heart yearns for all who are called by His holy name to take up the yoke of ministry, to carry the vessels of the Lord as priests of the Most High God in accord with God's call. May it be our heart's desire to be free to minister, serve, and worship in the fullness of Christ, and to administer the cups of saving grace to all who will receive. Let us cry out in earnest prayer for Christians to separate themselves from the things that keep us back and hold us down.

> *Therefore, since we are surrounded by such a great cloud of witnesses, let us throw off everything that hinders and the sin that so easily entangles. And let us run with perseverance the race marked out for us.*
>
> (Hebrews 12:1)

Running this race to the finish requires a great separation. We are given what is common to use for God's good purpose—to provide for our families in this temporal world. But to accomplish the work of the kingdom, we are called to rise above what is common, to separate from it, to enter into the power of Christ to worship, serve, and minister by the power of the Spirit of Jesus.

> *This is what the Lord says: "Cursed is the one who trusts in man, who depends on flesh for his strength."*
>
> (Jeremiah 17:5)

The wisdom of America's founding fathers applied the genius of this separation principle. The Old Testament prophets proclaimed the need for separating holy from common. The temple in Jerusalem was constructed in accord with God's plan to provide us with an illustration of walls and gates to separate the people to God who is holy, holy, holy.[6] As we build Scripture upon Scripture, we will see the presence of the Holy Spirit return like a mighty flood to anoint God's people to empower us to accomplish the impossible work set before us.

When we separate what is common from what is holy; we keep what is common for good and common purposes. At the same time, by means of the empowering work of the Spirit of Jesus, we accomplish what can only be done in the power and strength of the Spirit of a holy God. As we separate ourselves to what is holy, we escape the limitations of what is common and carry the vessels of the LORD to serve and minister in His kingdom. We step into the power that liberates us to minister, serve, and worship in a way that reveals the living, active presence of our LORD and Savior, Jesus Christ.

---

6. Isaiah 6:3, Revelation 4:8.

Chapter 10
The Benefits of Separation
Q & A

1. What happened after the "man whose appearance was like bronze" measured the temple to be sure holy and common were kept separated?

2. Why is separating holy from common an important truth in our day and time?

3. In the work of the kingdom of heaven, what is the benefit of separating holy from common?

My Journal Notes:

Chapter 11:
Pass Over the Thresholds

Key Scriptures:

- "And a highway will be there; it will be called the Way of Holiness; it will be for those who walk on that Way." (Isaiah 35:8)
- "These are the words of him who is holy and true, who holds the key of David. What he opens no one can shut, and what he shuts no one can open. I know your deeds. See, I have placed before you an open door that no one can shut." (Revelation 3:7–8)

A guardian cherub brandished a flaming sword to protect the way to the Tree of Life in the Garden of Eden.[1] After Adam and Eve ate the forbidden fruit, in violation of God's command, they were expelled from Eden's garden paradise. They were banished to earth's common realm where Adam would earn his way by sweat and labor. Death would reign over them and their descendants. The flaming sword in the angel's hand kept Adam, Eve, and all who would come after them from partaking of the fruit of the Tree of Life to live forever, leaving them estranged from God.

Are all of Adam's descendants forever banished, without hope? Is the fruit on the Tree of Life no longer available to humankind? Does the flaming sword of the angelic cherub drive everyone away? Certainly not! God is abundant in mercies. The flaming sword was not intended as a permanent barrier, but a threshold to be crossed. And our LORD Jesus provides the way.

In this chapter, we'll learn that there are many covenant thresholds in the kingdom of heaven. We'll expand and apply *what* we learned about fire as a threshold for those who are called to freedom in Christ—to Jesus who is the Tree of Life. We'll explore the significance of thresholds in God's kingdom and the good purpose they serve. This lesson prepares the learner for the next chapter, where we'll apply these truths to our everyday lives in preparation for an eternity with our heavenly Father

The angel with a flaming sword set up a guarded barrier to protect the way to the Tree of Life after Adam and Eve were banished. Many other kinds of barriers are recorded after this. Fortresses, walls, gates, doors, thresholds, veils, or curtains are in every book of the Bible. Ancient city gates were a place of welcome for friends of the city and a barrier for their enemies. Rebekah covered her face with a veil before Isaac came to meet her. The veil symbolized a

---

1. Genesis 3:24.

threshold that he could only cross over in a covenant of marriage.[2] In the same way, the flaming sword in an angel's hand remains as a test of fire to guarantee that those who pass over the threshold are in covenant with Christ. Jesus testified of Himself: I AM the way, I AM the door, I AM the gate. Jesus is not only the threshold; He is the Tree of Life that we seek. Jesus baptizes us with the Holy Spirit and with fire to make it possible for us to pass over and pass through the flames to partake of Christ.

When we receive the gift of saving faith, the lamp of our spirit lights up with the fire of the Holy Spirit. The fire burning in us is a refining fire, a fire that purifies, and a fire that surrounds us to prepare us to pass through the angel's flaming sword.

When you walk through the fire, you will not be burned; the flames will not set you ablaze.

(Isaiah 43:2)

When we receive Jesus' baptism of fire, we receive the oil of the Spirit of Jesus that fuels a fire in us. This fire empowers us in the service and ministry ordained for each one of us. In fire we are refined, prepared, and steeled against all fire as we work and wait for the full and complete revelation of Jesus Christ upon His return.

Notice the connection between the gifting and empowering work of the Holy Spirit, oil to keep the flame of your lamp burning, and the oil of the bridesmaids in Jesus' parable.[3] The Apostle Paul emphasizes this connection:

Therefore, you do not lack any spiritual gift as you eagerly wait for our Lord Jesus Christ to be revealed.

(1 Corinthians 1:7)

The five wise virgins in Jesus' parable kept an extra supply of oil as they waited and watched for the Bridegroom's return. The bridesmaid's oil was provided so their lamps would burn bright and drive away the darkness of night. This is the same oil the Spirit of Jesus uses to baptize us with the Holy Spirit and fire.[4] With Jesus' illustration as the standard, consider the Corinthian church that did not lack any spiritual gift (oil for the fire of the Spirit) as they waited for our Lord Jesus Christ to be revealed. The oil of the Spirit still burns in our hearts today to empower the Church. This is the oil that keeps the fire of our lamps burning to drive out the darkness as we wait for our Lord Jesus Christ's return when He will be fully revealed. Because this fire in us is the flame of the Spirit of Christ, we are made safe to cross the thresh-

---
2. Genesis 24:62–67.
3. Matthew 25:1–13.
4. Matthew 3:11.

old into God's holy, fiery presence. The angel's flaming sword remains as to guard the way to cross over and partake of the Tree of Life.

Blessed are those who wash their robes, that they may have the right to the tree of life and may go through the gates into the city.

(Revelation 22:14)

In Christ's baptism of fire, we are made ready to pass over the threshold for the final, great separation when everything is restored, death is defeated, and Christ Jesus is fully revealed. By means of Jesus' baptism in the Holy Spirit's fire, we are made ready to step through the fire unscathed. This is a threshold we must go through to partake of the fullness of the Tree of Life; the Bread of Life.

Because there is one bread, we who are many are one body, for we all partake of the one bread.

(1 Corinthians 10:17 ESV)

The significance of thresholds becomes evident as God's glory departed from the temple in Ezekiel chapter ten. Yehovah God paused at each door, gate, and threshold as if to water it with tears. Surely, the Lord yearned to find a repentant heart to whom He could show mercy. We cannot say for certain, but it would be consistent with God's long-suffering nature to stop, and wait, and search for someone who would intercede for His glory to remain in the temple that was built for His holy name. Why wouldn't the Almighty grieve? He knew they were so spiritually dead they would not even notice that His glory had departed.

Step by step, threshold by threshold, gate by gate, God's glory departed from His temple of worship. A vital check was called for at each threshold before passing over. Psalm 84:10 may be best translated from the original Hebrew as: "I would rather guard the threshold in the house of my God than dwell in the tents of evil." Meditating on this Scripture leads us to wonder if guards at the thresholds searched for "repentance," "thanksgiving," "intercessions," and "praise." Did God Almighty pause at each threshold for the watchmen to confirm: "There are no repentant hearts here?" Did God verify with each watchman at the gate that no hearts remained there to overflow with thanksgiving? Did God stop before He crossed over every threshold to verify with the gatekeeper that His covenant was broken, and the blood sacrifice of the covenant trampled upon? Did He search for someone to stand in the gap?

The prophet Ezekiel showed us the LORD Almighty as He crossed the thresholds and departed from the temple. Now witness God's splendor and majesty when He breaks through each threshold. He is mighty in battle, and no mountain or barrier will stand against Him.

When God called Isaiah to a holy work, the Lord broke through thresholds with might and power; shaking them to their foundation.[5] When the Great I AM delivered His people from slavery and brought them out of Egypt, the mountains shook and the hills leaped at His holy presence.[6] The mountains quaked when our LORD Jesus gave up His spirit, and died on the cross.

At that moment the curtain of the temple was torn in two from top to bottom. The earth shook, the rocks split.

(Matthew 27:51)

The Great I AM made a way for us to be brought before Him; no longer estranged by our sin and depravity. There is no other way than through Jesus Christ, whose blood is the threshold. Even if we had the strength of a horse prepared for battle, we could not depend upon our mortal power. Indeed, God Almighty threw horse and rider into the sea.[7] We don't have enough strength of our own to pass over the threshold. The prophet Jeremiah's hard words decried our human tendency to do by our own means:

This is what the Lord says: "Cursed is the one who trusts in man, who draws strength from mere flesh and whose heart turns away from the Lord."

(Jeremiah 17:5)

The collective human wisdom of Earth's greatest thinkers cannot break through the threshold Yehovah God established. Christian theologians delight in their studied interpretations of Scripture, reading from original scripts in Greek and Hebrew. This is excellent until it becomes the pride of man, because earthbound wisdom will be brought to nothing.

For the wisdom of this world is foolishness in God's sight. As it is written: "He catches the wise in their craftiness."

(1 Corinthians 3:19)

The greatest human strength, the collective wisdom of the world's great thinkers, and the remarkable power of humankind cannot breach the threshold of the angel's fiery sword. There is only one way to cross the threshold, and it is not by means of human might or mortal power.

---

5. Isaiah 6:4 ESV.
6. Psalm 114.
7. Exodus 15:21.

"Not by might nor by power, but by my Spirit," says the Lord Almighty.

(Zechariah 4:6)

The blood of the New Covenant, the blood of the Lamb, makes a better way for us to cross the threshold into a covenant relationship with Jesus Christ. By His blood shed on the cross, Jesus Christ provided a way for His glory to be revealed among His people. The cross of Jesus made a way to pass over the threshold.

Jesus comes to each of us, knocking on our heart's door so He may enter and speak with us around a table of fellowship. The blood of the Lamb of God must be applied with hyssop to the doorposts of our threshold, and the holy presence of the LORD will enter to break bread with us. The Psalmist wrote about the cleansing ability of hyssop:

Cleanse me with hyssop, and I will be clean; wash me, and I will be whiter than snow.

(Psalm 51:7)

The cleansing blood of the Lamb, applied to the doorposts above the threshold, provides a way for the LORD Almighty's presence to enter and fellowship with His bride. In the same way, there are thresholds to cross into God's presence. In the kingdom realm, this threshold is not a barrier, but a portal; a beginning point, the place where a spiritual reality takes effect, and the point at which truth becomes reality. David, the Psalmist, mused about thresholds:

Enter his gates with thanksgiving and his courts with praise;
give thanks to him and praise his name.

(Psalm 100:4)

Those whose souls overflow with thanksgiving, and whose lips flood out with praise, may enter the gates of God's presence. With voices lifted in praise, God's children are equipped to enter into the courts of worship in the heavenly realm. The Good Shepherd takes us in His arms to carry us over the threshold. In His loving arms, we are filled with thanksgiving and praise as we are brought into the beauty of God's majesty. Take a life-changing step, come as a bride adorned for her husband, and you will see the glory of His gathering place.

But you have come to Mount Zion, to the city of the living God, the heavenly Jerusalem. You have come to thousands upon thousands of angels in joyful assembly, to the church of the firstborn, whose names are written in heaven. You have come to God, the Judge of all, to the spirits of the righteous made perfect, to Jesus the mediator of a new covenant, and to the sprinkled blood that speaks a better word than the blood of Abel.

(Hebrews 12:22–24)

Jesus made a way so that we may pass over the threshold and come to Him—by means of His shed blood. As Jesus died on the cross, the veil in Jerusalem's temple was torn open to make a way for all who will come to the throne of grace.

Now, in Christ, in the fire of the Spirit of Jesus, there is a way for us to cross over the threshold into God's holy presence. With overflowing thanksgiving, we are ushered through the gates, and with praise we are brought into His courts. As we enter, we are separated from the burdens and distractions of this common realm and lifted into the realm of the kingdom of heaven.

All God's children look forward to the day when the New Jerusalem will descend upon earth. It's a walled city of awesome beauty with twelve gate thresholds, each guarded by an angel. The walls are made of jasper, and each gate will be a single pearl.[8] Three gates each face North, South, East, and West. It's as if each gate is set to receive what the four winds from the earth will bring from every continent on Earth. The wind of the Spirit of Jesus will call all whose names are written in the Book of Life to enter through heaven's gates. From every corner of the earth, from every tribe, nation, and culture, the wind of the Spirit will bring God's people, adorned as a bride, to His eternal dwelling place. Each gate is a threshold guarded by a holy angel so that we may be forever separated from the cause of tears, sorrow, and pain.

Nothing impure will ever enter it, nor will anyone who does what is shameful or deceitful, but only those whose names are written in the Lamb's book of life.

(Revelation 21:27)

The first Adam's fatal debt of sin passes on to all who are born after him. But we are not born into this world without hope because all who are born in Christ, all who are called by His holy name, are born in freedom—their debt fully paid. We pass through the fire of the guardian angel's sword and come to the Tree of life, who is Jesus, Messiah. We cross over this threshold to reach out and partake of life-giving fruit of the Vine. When we pass through this gate, we are separated to Yehovah God. We are made a holy people, called out of the darkness of this world into the light of Christ. Indeed, Our Lord Jesus Christ is the only way. He carries us across the threshold into God's abundant saving grace. Yeshua, our Savior, separates us from the destructive chaos of the world. He paid our debt of sin and takes us to partake of the Tree of Life.

---

8. Revelation 21:21.

But you are a chosen people, a royal priesthood, a holy nation, God's special possession, that you may declare the praises of him who called you out of darkness into his wonderful light.

(1 Peter 2:9)

Chapter 11
Pass Over the Thresholds
Q & A

1. What is the first guarded barrier in the Bible? Why was it set in place?

2. Describe a covenant threshold and its purpose.

3. What is the oil of the Holy Spirit? Describe its powerful effect in ministry, service, and worship.

4. How is it possible for the first Adam's descendants to come to the Tree of Life?

My Journal Notes:

Chapter 12:
Today and Forever

Key Scriptures:

- "I provide water in the wilderness and streams in the wasteland, to give drink to my people, my chosen, the people I formed for myself that they may proclaim my praise." (Isaiah 43:20–21)

- "But know that the Lord has set apart the godly for himself; the Lord hears when I call to him." (Psalm 4:3 ESV)

Let's come back down to earth where our lives are filled with separations of all kinds. In order for us to take our first breath, we had to be separated from our mother's womb, and then our umbilical cord was cut. When we started first grade, we were separated from everyday life at home with mom. After years of late-night study sessions, exams, and internships, a certificate of graduation was granted us—a passport to our future. Finally, we held in our hand a parchment paper neatly rolled and tied with a golden ribbon. We updated our resume to announce: "MBA graduate Summa cum Laude." With this paper in hand, we became separated from our scholarly and not-so-scholarly friends. It was time to get a real job, leave our home town, and separate from everything familiar.

Remember when you fell in love? Every minute you were separated from the love of your life was unbearable. You thought about your love as you drove to work. Your heart jumped at the thought of him as you tried to concentrate on your work. All day long, you looked for a way to talk your boss into letting you off early so you could be with your love. You could hardly wait until that moment you would both say, "I do," and the veil lifted for the first husband-and-wife kiss.

But when that anticipated moment arrived for you to be joined together, separations came with it. You had to move out of your bedroom at home. You had to give up the muscle car posters tacked to the walls, your Seahawks banners, and the rock collection you gathered on your childhood adventures. You had to separate yourself from the comforts of mom's cooking and dad's solid, steady wisdom. You had to disconnect from the security of your childhood home to make your own.

Now think about the Bridegroom, our Lord Jesus, who is preparing a place for you. He thinks of you every moment of the day and night. His presence surrounds you in everything you say and do. He knows your heart's desire and He is preparing a place for you to spend eternity with him. I can only imagine that when He carries you across the threshold into your forever residence you will look around and exclaim, "It is so beautiful! The color is perfect! How did you know this is what I would like?"

In that great day of the LORD, you will be separated from sorrow, from tears, from suffering, from worries, and from the burden of all your cares in this earthbound existence. You will be separated from the threat of war, mass shootings, political insanities, taxes, catastrophic illness, and the ruin of bankruptcy. You will be separated from the evils of this world, and you will spend eternity separated with your Bridegroom, Jesus Christ.

You will join Him in the victory over sin, death, and suffering. On the day all things are placed under Jesus' feet, a great and final victory will be won and you will join with Him in victorious celebration—a wedding celebration. This wedding celebration has been planned from the beginning of time. As God created all the heavens and earth, He began to make a way for this great and final victorious celebration.

Consider this truth next time you read the account of creation. Read the first two chapters in Genesis again and meditate on them to see that, in all God created, He separated one thing from another. God began on day one by separating light from darkness, and continued on day two, separating the waters above from the waters below. By day three, God separated the dry land from the sea. On the fourth day of creation, God separated day from night and season from season. The work of day five was to separate "the living creature that has life, and the birds that fly above the earth" from the waters of the sea. Day six was especially busy as God created every kind of living creature, separating them from the dust of the earth. Then Creator God made man in His likeness. He brought forth trees from the earth and nourished all seed-bearing plants. The great work of creation was completed, and then on day seven God separated Himself from the work of creation in a day of rest.

This was just the beginning of the mighty work God would complete among all He created. The great separations continued. In the Holy Scriptures, we're given many illustrations of separations that apply to us: wheat from chaff, and sheep from goats. Abraham was separated from his homeland. David was singled out; separated from his brothers to be made king over Israel. The prophet Ezekiel admonished the people to separate what is holy from what is common. And finally, in that great day of God's victory, the angels will be sent to gather the elect and separate even two men working side by side in a field and two women grinding together in the mill.[1]

---
1. Matthew 24:40–41.

This is how it will be at the end of the age.
The angels will come and separate the wicked from the righteous.

(Matthew 13:49)

On day one of creation, Father God began this good work to prepare the way for His victory over sin, Satan, and death. Now is the time to prepare yourself for Jesus' final victory. He holds out His hands with good gifts to prepare you as a bride for His return. You can be dressed and ready for this great day, and today is the best day to start getting ready. The prophet Isaiah compels those who carry the vessels of the LORD to separate themselves to Him.

Depart, depart, go out from there! Touch no unclean thing!
Come out from it and be pure, you who carry the articles of the Lord's house.

(Isaiah 52:11)

The message is clear for those who watch for the Bridegroom's return. In the Church, all Christians are called to serve as royal priests. This is the priesthood of all believers. This includes everyone who comes to saving faith in our LORD, Jesus Christ. None of Jesus' followers are excluded from this holy priesthood because of race, gender, or status. When we are redeemed by the blood of Jesus and anointed by the oil of the Spirit of Jesus, we are priests called to carry the holy vessels of worship before a Holy God. No one who is separated to Christ is excluded.

So in Christ Jesus you are all children of God through faith, for all of you who were baptized into Christ have clothed yourselves with Christ. There is neither Jew nor Gentile, neither slave nor free, nor is there male and female, for you are all one in Christ Jesus. If you belong to Christ, then you are Abraham's seed, and heirs according to the promise.

(Galatians 3:26–29)

What do the holy vessels contain? We carry the anointing oil of ministry, and this is the power for all gifts of the Spirit. These talents are given and empowered by the Holy Spirit for the purpose of worshipful ministries and service to God's people. Holy vessels filled with the oil of the Spirit make the eternal work of God's kingdom possible. As God's holy people, we are called to separate ourselves from what is common. This separation makes us a unique people who glorify the Lord Almighty in all we do.

God chose the foolish things of the world to shame the wise; God chose the weak things of the world to shame the strong. God chose the lowly things of this world and the despised things–and the things that are not–to nullify the things that are, so that no one may boast before him.

(1 Corinthians 1:27–29)

We can no longer depend on our own strength and power to minister and serve. This is a threshold we must cross—a separation that prepares us for the great separation as the bride of Christ Jesus, who is our Bridegroom.

Each of us must take the time to take account of our personal strengths, abilities, talents, experience, training, and education. Update our resume to be sure our achievements are evident. Look over the latest financial statement of all our personal assets. Consider all the things of value in life that have brought us to where we are today. Now, count all these things as nothing. Count them as worthless so that we, in mortal weakness, can step up to minister and serve in the power and strength of the Spirit—all for the glory and honor of the Lord Almighty as we wait and watch for the Bridegroom's return.

David the Psalmist wrote about the thresholds of thanksgiving and praise we pass over as we come before the Lord to minister, serve, and worship. To cross the threshold of the gates to the Lord Almighty's holy presence, we offer up a sacrifice of thanksgiving. We cast off the burdens and distractions of this common realm to step across the threshold to a place of reverent worship and to lift up an offering of praise. Each threshold is guarded to keep out thieves and robbers who attempt to cross over by means of human will or mortal strength.[2] Our sacrifice of thanksgiving and our offerings of praise are the work of the Holy Spirit of Jesus overflowing from the heart. Indeed, it is out of the abundance of our hearts that true praise, thanksgiving, and worship flow.

There are many thresholds to pass over in our lifetime here on terra firma. We crossed a threshold as we took our first breath and thresholds must be crossed almost daily until we breathe our last gasp of air. Without breath, our spirit and soul separate from our body to be present with the Lord.[3] In the spiritual realm, heaven's fire serves to prove, cleanse, and refine. The flames serve as thresholds to pass over to keep us from depending on our common strengths to do kingdom work. We cross a threshold to be made one in covenant with Jesus Christ, and a partaker of the Tree of Life. The gifting and empowering work of the Spirit of Jesus prepares us as God's vessels to cross a threshold into the fullness of Christ in our worship, service and ministry. In the Spirit, we are gifted with sufficient oil to keep the fire burning in us. Jesus' baptism with fire empowers us to fulfill our Great Commission call and prepares us to cross the threshold and enter the King's wedding feast of the Bridegroom.

---

2. Matthew 22:1–4.
3. 2 Corinthians 5:8.

Chapter 12
Today and Forever
Q & A

1. What is in the holy vessels we carry, and what is its purpose?

2. Describe the heart of the Bridegroom toward His bride.

3. What will you be separated from on the "Day of the Lord"?

4. Who is included in the priesthood of believers?

My Journal Notes:

Chapter 13:
The Finish Line in Sight

Key Scriptures:

- "Whoever has ears, let them hear what the Spirit says to the churches. To the one who is victorious, I will give the right to eat from the tree of life, which is in the paradise of God." (Revelation 2:7)

- "Look, I am coming soon! My reward is with me, and I will give to each person according to what they have done. I am the Alpha and the Omega, the First and the Last, the Beginning and the End." (Revelation 22:12–13)

As we read historical Bible passages, we see that God works through whomever He chooses, and by whatever means He desires. As an example, God called Cyrus, a common king, to wreak God's judgment upon idolatrous Jerusalem. God's purpose was to restrain sin in His people and bring them back into fellowship. In our lifetimes, we have witnessed God's justice at work through various means. Quite often, He has worked through what is common to accomplish His good purpose and plan. The fight for genuine racial and gender equality falls into this category. God has used common means, and has inspired good and godly people to push forward on many fronts. This cause had a good beginning, but God isn't finished with us yet.

God desires to work justice and righteousness on the earth and this is a good time to join with Him in this good work. But this work of grace will not be fully accomplished by common means, and it is time for us to separate from common efforts alone and enter into the fullness of Christ.

For the task before us, we must not make the mistake of relying on spirituality found in the beauty of the earth, or in common life that surrounds us. The birth of a child, baby robins in a nest, the first time a couple hold hands, a walk on the beach as the sun sets, a shared meal with friends, the first daffodil of spring, or the first tomato you pick in your garden; these precious moments feel genial and even spiritual, and yet they are not holy. They are not sacramental. They are God's good and common gifts to humankind. In our day, as the finish line for the Great Commission race comes into view, it is time to step up in a strength that is not our own.

Those who hope in the Lord will renew their strength. They will soar on wings like eagles;
they will run and not grow weary, they will walk and not be faint.

(Isaiah 40:31)

It is time to catch a second wind and run in the strength and power of the Spirit of Jesus. Today the Good Shepherd calls us to minister, serve, and worship by means of what is holy—by the power and gifts of the Spirit. God is calling us to cross the threshold from what is common to what is holy. Then God's glory will fill our temple and confirm the truth of the Resurrected Christ who is alive and actively present.

> *And so it was with me, brothers and sisters.*
> *When I came to you, I did not come with eloquence or human wisdom as I proclaimed to you the testimony about God. For I resolved to know nothing while I was with you except Jesus Christ and him crucified. I came to you in weakness with great fear and trembling. My message and my preaching were not with wise and persuasive words, but with a demonstration of the Spirit's power, so that your faith might not rest on human wisdom, but on God's power.*
> (1 Corinthians 2:1–5)

Today, we are called to count our natural gifts as nothing. In the realm of God's kingdom, our talents, abilities, training, diplomas, degrees, and our impressive resumes add up to zero. Instead, we are compelled to depend upon the Spirit of Jesus and His mighty, powerful presence that indwells us. We are called to shine out His glorious light that pushes back the darkness in people's lives. We are to build upon the Foundation, Jesus Christ, with "gold, silver, and costly stones"[1] that will pass the test of fire.

The people of the ancient tribes of Israel turned away from God to worship and serve idols of wood, stone, silver, and gold. They even brought their idols into God's temple, where they worshiped these inanimate objects. It's as if they faced one way to worship an idol, and then turned around to worship the Creator of all heaven and earth. Today's idolatry is not so evident as a carved block of wood or a chiseled stone statue, but modern Christians, like them, bring our idolatry right into houses of prayer and worship.

Our idolatry is of the covert variety and begins in a most benign way. When Christians minister and serve by means of their God-given natural or common gifts and talents alone, it feels right and good—pleasing to us in every way. God does use people in the space they're in, but Christians risk falling into self-reliance when we depend on ourselves to do the kingdom work we are called to do. The prophet Hosea warned God's people with these words:

> *Because you have depended on your own strength and on your many warriors,*
> *the roar of battle will rise against your people.*
> (Hosea 10:13–14)

---
1. 1 Corinthians 3:12.

Reliance on our own strength quickly grows into self-confidence, escalates into feeling self-assured, and then turns into an idolatry of self. This false worship infects too many of our Christian gatherings in the modern-day church. We are called to put aside anything that will hold us back and then minister and serve in His name.

Therefore, since we are surrounded by such a great cloud of witnesses, let us throw off everything that hinders and the sin that so easily entangles. And let us run with perseverance the race marked out for us.

(Hebrews 12:1)

This kind of ministry requires pruning to make the branches of the vine productive again. The season for pruning is now. The trimming prepares the Church to produce a crop of abundant fruit. We are being called to repent and turn from the idolatry of self because our heavenly Father is worthy of all glory. The prophet Isaiah spoke what God was speaking, and God's word for the church has not changed.

I will not yield my glory to another or my praise to idols.

(Isaiah 42:8)

The prophet continued to exhort God's people with these encouraging words:

Depart, depart, go out from there! Touch no unclean thing! Come out from it and be pure, you who carry the articles of the Lord's house.

(Isaiah 52:11)

Isaiah wrote these words for all who carry the vessels of worship. In Isaiah's time, his words were for the priests who ministered and served in the LORD's temple. Today his words speak to the priesthood of all believers; that is, all who are called by the name of our LORD, Jesus Christ. It's vital that we answer the call to separate ourselves from doing the work of the Great Commission by common means and natural gifts. The need for separation is too powerful and effective to brush aside.

When we use what is common in an attempt to accomplish the work of the Spirit, we steal away from the glory due Almighty God. This is because His power is best manifested in weakness. How does this play out in real life service and ministry? When a pastor, prophet, teacher, minister, or evangelist speaks by means of their own intellect and by studied interpretations alone, the effect is limited. When we teach, preach, prophesy, evangelize, or minister by means of the gifts and power of the Spirit of Jesus, we become ministering vessels filled with the power and authority of the Spirit. Indeed, when God's people accomplish in the Spirit what they cannot accomplish by common means, God receives all the glory. We are compelled to step up to the call and run the race by means of the Spirit of Jesus.

> *I press on toward the goal to win the prize*
> *for which God has called me heavenward in Christ Jesus.*
>
> (Philippians 3:14)

Let's lighten our load and throw off the weights that drag us down so that we can run this Great Commission race. This is right and good in every way. The prophet Zechariah spoke out with this important message and we must hear it, and hear it again so we can live and serve according to this truth:

> *This is the word of the Lord to Zerubbabel:*
> *"Not by might nor by power, but by my Spirit," says the Lord Almighty.*
>
> (Zechariah 4:6)

The angel of the LORD spoke these words as he showed the prophet a candlestick with seven channels of light that burned with oil from the two olive trees beside it. The Holy Spirit is the source of the miraculous oil. Likewise, the work of building the temple of a holy God would not be accomplished by the strength of men, but through the Spirit of God who stirred them up, to encourage and strengthen them in body and spirit to do the work set before them.

The church began on the day of Pentecost by means of an outpouring of the Holy Spirit upon those who were gathered to pray and wait upon the Lord as commanded. The fire and gifts of the Spirit of Christ came with a mighty wind, given to establish the church. The work of the church was then carried forward by the power of the Spirit, and must be carried forward in our day in this same power.

King Saul offers an example of this failure: the sin of rebellion brought his reign to an end and we can learn from his mistakes. The prophet Samuel instructed the king to wait for him where Israel's armies were camped. Then Samuel would offer a sacrifice to the LORD before Israel went into battle. But King Saul's warriors were scattering, hiding in caves and deserting the ranks because they feared their enemy. Saul's anxious thoughts tempted him to begin the fight before they all went home. Rather than wait, he became impatient and offered a sacrifice to the LORD on his own. That sounds like a good thing to do, right? But this was in direct conflict with what God's prophet instructed him to do.[2] The seed of his wrongful act began simple enough, with an anxious, self-focused attitude.

---
2. 1 Samuel 13:7--10.

We are just as impatient as King Saul. We are people of action. We're quick to take the bull by the horns and make things happen. Jesus' commandment to wait falls on deaf ears. What are we waiting for? The empowering and gifting work of the Holy Spirit.

> *Do not leave Jerusalem, but wait for the gift my Father promised, which you have heard me speak about.*
>
> (Acts 1:4)[3]

We cannot do the work of the church, the kingdom of heaven, or the Great Commission in the power of mortal man. We must wait upon the LORD for His Spirit to gift and empower us for battle. To charge forward on our own, in our own strength, to do the work of the church will sow seeds that can sprout up in rebellion. This was king Saul's great downfall. The attitude of his heart led to disobedience, which led him into full-fledged rebellion.

> *For rebellion is as the sin of divination, and insubordination is as iniquity and idolatry. Because you have rejected the word of the Lord, He has also rejected you.*
>
> (1 Samuel 15:23 ESV)

We must not be like King Saul. Too often we are impatient and jump into work, service, and ministries on our own, apart from the gifts and power of the Spirit of Jesus. Instead, we are called to wait upon the Spirit of the LORD, to bind ourselves to the LORD, and to adhere to the LORD.

> *Wait for the Lord; be strong and take heart and wait for the Lord.*
>
> (Psalm 27:14)[4]

The work of the Holy Spirit is too often confused by various Christian denominations today. But the truth is simple, and there is no need for confusion. Those who come to saving faith in Jesus Christ receive the gift of the Holy Spirit to seal them from God's holy wrath for the day they will enter

---

[3]. The work of the Holy Spirit is too often confused by various Christian denominations today. But the truth is simple, and there is no need for confusion. Those who come to saving faith in Jesus Christ receive the gift of the Holy Spirit to seal them from God's holy wrath for the day they will enter into God's eternal glory. But the Holy Spirit isn't finished with His work in a believer's life. As an example: The Holy Spirit continues to work to convince and convict of sin—not all at once or we would be overwhelmed. Little by little, by the power of God's word and the Holy Spirit, we come to see our sin, confess our sin, and receive Jesus' cleansing from our sin. The Holy Spirit is also active and present in the sanctification of the saints. But the Holy Spirit has even more for God's children. For ministries and service in the church, and the Great Commission, we must wait and receive the gifts and power of the Spirit of Jesus so that we may accomplish all God has purposed and planned for us to do. The Holy Spirit's work in a Christian's life is continuous, abundant, and multifaceted. We are an impoverished people when we leave out any part of the work of Christ.

[4]. The Hebrew word for "wait" is קָוָה *qavah*. This is not an inactive waiting, but a time for binding ourselves to the LORD.

into God's eternal glory. But the Holy Spirit isn't finished with His work in a believer's life. As an example: The Holy Spirit continues to work to convince and convict of sin—not all at once or we would be overwhelmed. Little by little, by the power of God's word and the Holy Spirit, we come to see our sin, confess our sin, and receive Jesus' cleansing from our sin. The Holy Spirit is also active and present in the sanctification of the saints. But the Holy Spirit has even more for God's children. For ministries and service in the Church, and the Great Commission, we must wait and receive the gifts and power of the Spirit of Jesus so that we may accomplish all God has purposed and planned for us to do. The Holy Spirit's work in a Christian's life is continuous, abundant, and multifaceted. We are an impoverished people when we leave out any part of the work of Christ.

There is no need for us to be like the Galatian church. In the Apostle Paul's letter, he used some strong language to admonish them for going back to their old way of depending on their own resources. They started out great but then tripped over their own feet.

Are you so foolish?
After beginning by means of the Spirit, are you now trying to finish by means of the flesh?
(Galatians 3:3)

The Galatians were true to the Gospel when they first came to saving faith. Their ministry and service were powerful proof of this. But they slipped into default mode and began to worship and serve in the strength of the flesh. This was a backwards attempt to earn God's favor. Like the Galatians, the Church today has weakened itself in their effort to do the work of the Great Commission by means of human effort—by means of our common gifts and talents. We run and become weary. We walk and become faint. We fall down when God would lift us up and empower us to soar as on the wings of eagles.

This default mode comes to us quite naturally. One of Jesus' awesome moments with his disciples was Peter's confession: "You are the Christ." But moments later, Jesus had to rebuke him, saying, "Get behind me, Satan." It's like Peter tumbled from a moment of great revelation by means of the Spirit into a moment of common thinking. We, like Peter, are subject to this common weakness.

When we carry the holy vessels for service and ministry, we put aside what is common, and become God's holy instruments. It is only by means of the Holy Spirit's power that we can finish this Great Commission marathon. To do so by means of our common gifts and talents is like using unauthorized fire.[5] We are called to put aside self-reliance to become God-reliant. We must give up on self-empowerment to become Spirit-empowered. We do not minister and serve by means of self-assurance, but minister in the assurance of our Lord, Jesus Christ. Christians ought to no longer be self-confident, but God-confident. We will no longer be independent, but serve under authority.

> *For in him the whole fullness of deity dwells bodily,*
> *and you have come to fullness in him, who is the head of every ruler and authority.*
>
> (Colossians 2:9–10 NRSV)

The Apostle Paul compelled all who will carry the vessels of service to separate themselves from ministering before the Lord by any other means than the Holy Spirit's gifts and power. We are called to separate ourselves from the "sweat of our brow" as we fulfill our calling. The reason is simple. Sweat came with the curse of sin, and those who do the work of God's kingdom are free from this curse. In this freedom, our load is lightened so we can run the Great Commission race in the power of the Spirit.

As an example, listen to the beautiful music played on a flute. It's a delightful instrument that offers a flutter of notes to calm the soul and inspire the heart. This music can put a dance in our step. But the flute is only an instrument in the hands of the musician. If the instrument began to think of itself as a master flutist to play its own composition, it would no longer be useful in the hands of a musician. The flute must separate from its own desires and then play a beautiful song with the wind of flutist—this is a great separation. Our natural body and our common gifts and abilities cannot accomplish the eternal work of God's kingdom. Our Lord and Master, by means of spiritual gifts and His Spirit's power, will accomplish His eternal purpose and plan—like instruments in the Master's hand.

In the book of Acts, the church leaders chose seven who were "full of the Spirit and wisdom" to serve and wait tables.[6] Why was it so important to have people who were gifted and empowered in the Spirit to put on an apron and wait tables? A real-life example may complete the picture for us. If the church needed a chef to manage the kitchen for summer camp, they would look for someone with appropriate skills. The chef would need to have experience in restaurant kitchen management, staff training, recipe and menu creation, nutrition, staff leadership, food safety, sanitation, cost control, and purchasing. If this camp were secular, this would be enough, because these are common qualifications for the work of getting healthy food in front of the kids that they will eat and enjoy.

---

5. Leviticus 10:1.
6. Acts 6:2–3.

But when Christians gather around a table to share a meal, it's about more than food that is enjoyable and nourishing for the body. There is a bond of fellowship in "breaking bread" together. There is a miraculous element to sharing a meal with thanksgiving "in Christ."[7] We are brought together in a bond of family and friendship that is stronger than a best-friend-at-summer-camp relationship. This miracle of a familial bond with eternal effect around the table is only possible by means of the presence of Christ and the Holy Spirit at work through those he chooses to use in this great mission. The camp chef needs all the experience listed above, but the greatest qualification must be the garment of ministry that is only possible by the power and gifts of the Spirit of Jesus.

We are commissioned to go forward to do the work of the Great Commission by means of, in the strength of, and the gifts and power of the Spirit of Jesus. Apart from the fire burning in us that is fueled by the oil of the Spirit and driven by the wind of the Spirit, this work is impossible. In the strength of mortal men or women the work will never be accomplished. To carry out this good work with eternal effect, we must overcome our inclination to default to common mode.

Will you answer the call? Will your strength be renewed like the eagles? Will you run the race? Will you separate yourself from the weakness of the common realm, and be separated to the power and strength of the Spirit of Jesus to carry the vessels of ministry and service? Will you wait and pray to be clothed in the garment of ministry—the gifts and power of the Spirit of Jesus? Will you minister and serve to accomplish the work of the church, the Great Commission, and the kingdom of heaven to change lives for all eternity?

---

7. A shared meal like this does not detract from the LORD's Table, i.e. Communion. Instead it can serve an appetizer. A dinner gathering, in Christ, whets our appetite for the LORD's Table.

"To preach the gospel, and not with words of eloquent wisdom, lest the cross of Christ be emptied of its power."
The Apostle Paul[8]

---

8. 1 Corinthians 1:17 ESV.

Chapter 13
The Finish Line in Sight
Q & A

1. Why is the call to separate holy from common so important for Christians today?

2. Describe idolatry in the modern-day church.

3. When God said, "I will not give my glory to another," speaking through Isaiah, what is the thrust of His words?

4. What is the end result when we get impatient and refuse to wait on the Lord?

My Journal Notes:

Postscript:

After finishing the first draft of this study guide, I took time to reflect on the message of this project and its application to my own life. Writing this manuscript required a lot of digging in the Scriptures, and I've drawn much closer to my heavenly Father. As I became closer to the Lord Almighty, a dark corner in my own heart became evident, and God was once again faithful to show me my sin, convince me of my sin, convict me, and then separate me from the darkness of my sin through forgiveness.

I was compelled to confess and grieve over my sin and come to Jesus Christ to be forgiven and cleansed. As I'm writing this, the burden is lifted and the LORD is restoring to me the joy of my salvation.

It's a good lesson for me and for all of my family in Christ. When we teach truths from the Scriptures, God is faithful to His Word to make the truths we teach a reality in our own lives. Confession is good for the soul, and God is faithful to forgive and cleanse.

My goal, as always, is to write worthy words, true words, refreshing words, inspiring words, and healing words to refresh the soul.

Acknowledgments:

A finished book is never the work of one person working alone. The fellowship, teaching, and accountability of my family of faith have been a crucial part of this effort. My wife, Susie, has stood with me through the thick and thin of research, study, writing, rewriting, and editing this study book. A lot of research notes went back and forth between myself and my good friend Mark Philpot, who works with me on Biblical Hebrew and Semitic viewpoints. My great friend Jeff Kincaid patiently answered my theological questions. His answers begin with complex depth, and then boil down to clear truths centered in Christ. Also, my fellow writers at Word Weavers have offered excellent writing tips and critiques of my work.

About the Author

A wide and varied education in the doctrines and theologies of the church have been an important part of Cho Larson's training. His instruction began on his mother's lap, as she read Bible stories. And then, from the day Cho began to walk by faith in Jesus Christ, God has given him a heart to search the Scriptures to prove or disprove what he heard preached and taught. One thing has been constant in his training: the Spirit of Jesus has been a compass to keep him on the right path. Because his Bible training included growing up in and attending Nazarene, Evangelical United Brethren, Free Methodist, Christian Reformed, Dutch Reformed, Pentecostal, Assemblies of God, Baptist, and the Advent Christian church,[9] this strong compass was necessary.

The Spirit of the Lord jarred him awake spiritually using the anointed preaching of Pastor Starr at a Baptist church in Spokane Valley when he was caught up in a life of selfish sin. God brought him into an Assemblies church, led him to a Vineyard Fellowship, Calvary Chapel, Disciples of Christ, and an LCMS Lutheran church. When Cho was a teenager, his dad was called to pastor a small Advent Christian church in Spokane, Washington. At the same time, Cho was very active in a local Youth for Christ that was led by many Baptists. There were a lot of conflicting messages.

Cho remembers that each of these churches taught the essential truths regarding Christ's saving grace, but their doctrines beyond that varied widely. Some taught more truth than others. He watched in agony as one of his churches effectively destroyed the faith of many believers who were not spiritually strong, when the pastor taught them to have faith in their faith. Cho has heard Word Faith teaching, hellfire preaching, all-you-need-is-love sermons, inspirational pep talks, moralistic lectures, self-help messages, and good-old-fashioned gospel preaching. All too often, Cho cringed under the preaching of false doctrines that didn't set right in his spirit, compelling him to search God's word to learn that what was taught was not true when tested by the whole of God's word.

Cho has read, researched, and tested the writings of Martin Luther, Matthew Henry, Watchman Nee, Dietrich Bonhoeffer, C.S. Lewis, A.W. Tozer, R.A. Torrey, R.C. Sproul, Charles Spurgeon, John Calvin, Dallas Willard, Billy Graham, Hank Hanegraaff, Wayne Grudem, Charles Swindoll, studied *The Book of Concord*, and too many other books and authors to list.

9. The Advent Christian Church is a Sunday-worshipping Adventist church.

Cho doesn't recommend these various forms of worship, training and education because it can be confusing. Too often, the conflict of teachings will erode one's faith. But God was always faithful to accomplish His good purpose, spurring him to check and recheck, search and research, and test every word that was taught.

In weakness, and from the mixed messages of his theological training, God has brought about a good work—all for His honor and glory. "God's power is manifested in weakness." The author's prayer is that his readers will test these written words using the holy Scripture as the standard.

Cho and his wife live in Northern Arizona's Verde Valley.

"May God bless you and keep you, and may you grow in grace and knowledge until you come to the fullness of Christ–inseparable from Christ."

www.ingramcontent.com/pod-product-compliance
Lightning Source LLC
Chambersburg PA
CBHW072015110526
44592CB00012B/1320